Teaching Assistant Strategies

Teaching Assistant Strategies

An Introduction to College Teaching

R. R. Allen
Theodore Rueter

KENDALL/HUNT PUBLISHING COMPANY
2460 Kerper Boulevard   P.O. Box 539   Dubuque, Iowa 52004-0539

Cover photo by Michael Kienitz,
Madison, Wisconsin

Contents

Preface

Teaching Assistant Strategies: An Introduction to College Teaching is intended for those who are, or who are about to be, teaching assistants. While it may be of interest to a wider readership, including deans, professors, and undergraduate students, it is to the specific TA audience that this book is addressed. With this special audience in mind, the authors are direct and, at times, irreverent. For example, professors are sometimes viewed as bosses or overseers rather than as revered mentors. While this may seem an ignoble view of the professorial class, it is a realistic view from a graduate teaching assistant's perspective.

Graduate students have special needs. A college department is a highly political environment consisting of strata of prestige and influence. Graduate students are in the bottom stratum. They continue as graduate students at the will of the professorial class. They must prove themselves as students over and over again as each semester unfolds and as benchmark moments threaten.

As graduate students assume the role of teaching assistants, their problems are compounded. They must now prove themselves as both students and teachers. While an appointment as a teaching assistant affords "heady status" to a bruised graduate student ego, it does not ensure competence in the newly assigned role. Many departments assume that bright graduate students will be competent college instructors. Although anyone who has attended a university has cause to doubt the veracity of this assumption, those who make decisions in college departments often continue to assume that budding scholars are, by nature, effective teachers. In this belief, many departments choose to ignore direct instruction in teaching methods in favor of the notion that bright people learn to teach by teaching. While TAs must be well grounded in their disciplines, they must also acquire insights about effective teaching. Fortunately, the training of teaching assistants is receiving increased attention throughout the academic community.

Teaching Assistant Strategies: An Introduction to College Teaching advances the point of view that the effectiveness of TAs may be improved through self-reflection, information about teaching, and adjustments in teaching practices. The first three chapters are introductory in nature. Chapter 1, "The Graduate Student as Teaching Assistant," considers teaching assistantships both from historical and contemporary perspectives and describes the benefits and challenges of the TA system. Chapter

2, "TA Roles and Styles," examines the process through which graduate students try out and become comfortable with varying teaching roles as they choose a teaching style that is both comfortable and effective. Chapter 3, "Interpersonal Relationships," considers the problems TAs face as they seek to relate to students, course directors, and members of the support staff.

The remaining chapters in the book consider areas of competence that all successful teaching assistants must master. Chapter 4, "Planning for Instruction," introduces TAs to the myriad of skills they must possess if they are to engage in effective instructional planning. Chapter 5, "Creating a Supportive Classroom Environment," offers suggestions for creating a positive atmosphere in the classroom. Chapter 6, "Lecturing," considers how TAs can make their lectures and other class presentations interesting and relevant. Chapter 7, "Leading Class Discussions," identifies the skills necessary to conduct productive class discussions. Chapter 8, "Facilitating Student Learning," considers the responsibilities associated with conducting autonomous skill development courses, teaching individuals, and directing laboratory sections. Chapter 9, "Assessing Student Learning," explains what a TA must know in order to measure and evaluate student progress. Chapter 10, "Growing in Teaching Skill," provides advice about external assessment and careful self-assessment. Taken as a whole, this book offers graduate students a forthright and practical introduction to college teaching as they anticipate and assume the responsibilities normally assigned to teaching assistants.

RRA
TAR

Acknowledgments

We have incurred many debts in the preparation of this book. We would like to thank JoAnne Allen, Lloyd Bitzer, Judith Craig, Lisa Dziadulewicz, Booth Fowler, Lisa Glueck, Erik Pages, and Nancy Westphal for reading portions of this manuscript and for providing friendly advice. We also appreciate the cooperation of the many presidents, chancellors, and deans who provided TA manuals as well as other information about TA programs and policies on their campuses. The research assistance of Porter Ball, Tip Blish, Daniel Curtis, Jay Dunn, and Robin Rhodes of Middlebury College is sincerely appreciated as is the secretarial assistance of Mary Dodge, Evelyn Miller, and Kriss Viney of the Department of Communication Arts, University of Wisconsin–Madison. Finally, we wish to thank Karla Rahn for taking the photographs that appear in this book.

1

The Graduate Student as Teaching Assistant

"The teaching assistant is a unique phenomenon of the modern, major research university, because the TA is simultaneously both a teacher and a student. Teaching assistants play a crucial role in the university's mission, by providing quality instruction. . . . [T]hey serve in a great variety of ways. They staff quiz and laboratory sections, they teach everything from freshman mathematics to foreign languages, and they assist the faculty in various other important tasks. For these reasons, it is essential that we appoint the most outstanding students as teaching assistants. I believe the TA system is a good one, for while we're doing all this we're helping students to finance their education, and we're also providing a training ground for the next generation of university faculty."[1]

Gene L. Woodruff
Dean of the Graduate School
University of Washington

Although TAs are an absolutely vital part of the instructional staff of many universities, graduate students often arrive on campus with only a vague notion of their functions and responsibilities. The purpose of this chapter and this book is to inform you about the TA experience. It begins by considering teaching assistantships both from historical and contemporary perspectives. The benefits of the TA system and the challenges faced by individual TAs are then examined.

Teaching Assistantships in Perspective

Teaching assistantships originated in the nineteenth century and have become increasingly prevalent with the passage of time. While known by varying titles, teaching assistants are an established institution in contemporary American universities.

History of Teaching Assistantships

Teaching assistantships in American universities arose out of a need to attract capable students to graduate school.[2] Richard Storr, in his account of the beginnings of graduate study in America, notes that after 1850 there was general agreement among educators that love of knowledge was not a sufficient inducement for students to enter graduate school; financial incentives were also necessary.[3] Even after this agreement in principle, the actual provision of graduate financial support was not immediately forthcoming.

Apparently the first successful large-scale effort to fund graduate education followed the founding of Johns Hopkins University in 1876. Hopkins President Daniel C. Graham's plan was to recruit outstanding graduate students by awarding twenty fellowships a year. Clark University and the University of Chicago soon imitated the Hopkins plan for supporting doctoral students.[4] Although these fellowships required no service in return, their amount ($400 to $500 a year) was not always sufficient for student needs; therefore, students on fellowship, including Woodrow Wilson at Johns Hopkins,[5] took to moonlighting. Such moonlighting established a precedent for and a transition to "lecturing to undergraduates—in all probability the origin of the TA system."[6]

The use of graduate students as teaching assistants "became a familiar feature of most graduate schools during the last decade or so of the nineteenth century."[7] Even at that time, a teaching assistantship offered a substantial challenge. One former Harvard graduate student reminisced about his single year of service in the following way:

> After spending a year in graduate study at Harvard, I was appointed by President Elliot Instructor in English . . . I read and marked over 700 themes a week—most of them were short themes, but some were not. Whenever I entered my room, I was greeted by the high pile of themes on the table, awaiting my attention. I read very few books the

whole year—there was no time. I never went to bed before midnight. With the highest respect and admiration for my colleagues, nothing on earth would have induced me to continue such brain-fagging toil another year.[8]

Fortunately, most contemporary TAs are not expected to engage in "brain-fagging toil."

Although the teaching assistantship system was rooted in the nineteenth century, the full flowering of the system awaited the growth of the undergraduate population following World War II. At that time, a wave of returning veterans—two million strong—flooded college campuses, while taking advantage of the GI Bill. By 1956, the United States government had spent around $5.5 billion on higher education benefits for veterans.[9]

To meet this massive influx of undergraduate students, many universities dramatically increased the size of their graduate departments in order to increase the corps of available teaching assistants. By so doing, "the undergraduate school . . . was able to obtain a greater amount of service per dollar from graduate students than from regularly qualified instructors."[10]

The federal government's response to the launch of Sputnik in the late 1950s provided an additional impetus for the growth of the TA system: "In the fields of perceived national shortages, massive funds were made available in the form of research assistantships, fellowships, and traineeships."[11] Graduate students were needed to fill these federally funded appointments as well as to staff teaching assistant positions. In addition to increasing the number of graduate students in many programs, the new funds were the source of increased tension. Chase observes that:

> The terms of these awards were, in most cases, so attractive that the well-established teaching assistantship came to be regarded as a second- or third-rate appointment. The inevitable result was that problems of morale developed among TAs—problems which commanded the attention of departmental chairmen, deans, and other administrative officers.[12]

To an extent, the problems caused by perceived status differences are with us still.

The demands for graduate student labor continued to grow in the 1960s and beyond. The move toward the "Great Society" brought federal research dollars into a number of departments and eventually into the pockets of graduate students who were employed as research assistants. The Higher Education Act of 1965 ensured that the undergraduate population would remain large by providing Educational

Opportunity Grants and Guaranteed Student Loans for college attendance. In 1972, Congress amended the law to provide direct entitlements to needy students. The Middle Income Student Act of 1978 expanded the eligibility of federal loans and grants, certifying the federal government's role in encouraging college attendance among the middle class as well as the poor.[13] In 1981, the United States Department of Education alone provided over $6 billion in federal student aid.[14] By 1986, this figure had risen to $9.4 billion annually.[15]

In the 1960s it was not possible to hire assistant professors quickly enough to meet the needs of an expanding student population. In the academic year 1962–63, for example, there were approximately a thousand fewer holders of doctorates available than were necessary to meet the demands of American universities.[16] To compensate for this shortfall, universities expanded their staffs by hiring great numbers of graduate students as teaching assistants. Resident degree-credit college enrollment rose from 3,215,544 in 1959–60 to 12,096,895 in 1980–81.[17] Similarly, the estimated "part-time, junior instructional staff" rose from 32,000 in 1960 to 140,000 in 1982.[18]

The Current Status of Teaching Assistantships

The terms teaching assistant and TA are generic rather than specific. Other titles frequently used are assistant lecturers, assistant instructors, readers, laboratory assistants, proctors, graduate teaching assistants, teaching fellows,[19] and graduate service assistants (who perform such duties as "clerical work, classroom and laboratory supervision, laboratory development and other similar duties which do not primarily involve teaching or research").[20] Berkeley uses the title GSI (graduate student instructors),[21] and Princeton refers to TAs as assistants in instruction, or AIs.[22]

There are also distinctions regarding levels of experience and responsibility. The University of Texas at Austin differentiates between teaching assistants and assistant instructors (the latter having independent responsibility for a course).[23] The University of Wisconsin–Madison distinguishes between "experienced" and "inexperienced" TAs. It also has "head TAs" in large, multisection courses, who are responsible for exam and problem set coordination or supervision. Graduate students who are ABDs (all but dissertation) are often employed as lecturers to teach elementary or intermediate courses. At UCLA, TA appointment and advancement are determined by "academic status, performance, prior experience, scholarship, and promise as a teacher."[24] UCLA has three levels of teaching assistants, based primarily on years of graduate study: teaching assistants, teaching associates, and teaching fellows. A teaching associate is simply a more experienced teaching assistant; a teaching fellow, like Texas' assistant instructor, is "expected to be able to provide the entire instruction of a low division course" under the direction of a supervising faculty member.[25]

TAs are overwhelmingly concentrated in large universities, with a relatively small proportion in liberal arts colleges and technological schools. They perform a wide variety of functions and roles in the university:

> The responsibilities of teaching assistants assigned by departments or programs may include but are not limited to such items as preparation for classes, preparation of audio-visual materials, leading discussions and supervising laboratories, attending lectures, rating student work, holding office hours and other consultations with students, writing and grading tests and examinations, compiling bibliographies, and conferring with the supervising professor. Teaching assistants also regularly participate in the Assignment Committee during registration periods, prepare laboratory materials, operate instructional equipment, and perform other instructionally related tasks.[26]

TAs are, in sum, a vital part of the academic life of the departments and universities employing them.

Epstein has noted that teaching assistants normally function in one of four ways: the assistant in the literal sense, who helps the professor by handing out materials, grading examinations, and performing other duties; the laboratory assistant, particularly in natural science courses; the discussion section leader; and the independent teacher of the tool subjects of English composition, foreign languages, mathematics, and speech communication.[27]

Undergraduates at major research universities are almost certain to encounter every type of TA during their undergraduate careers, as TAs are a ubiquitous presence on large college campuses. For example, at the University of California–Berkeley, teaching assistants are responsible for 58 percent of lower-division class meetings.[28]

Benefits of the TA System

The TA system has survived and prospered as a means of instructing undergraduate students for a number of reasons. In this section six advantages will be considered.

Helps Finance Graduate Education

TAs are usually appointed initially on an interim basis, with renewal for up to four or more years. TAships make graduate study economically more feasible for the tens of thousands of teaching assistants in American universities. TA pay varies across universities and often across departments in universities, based on supply and demand. The general salary range for half-time TAs is $6,000 to $10,000.[29] The handling of tuition for TAs also varies from campus to campus. In some public universities, out-of-state tuition is waived. In other universities, tuition may be totally excused. The handling of tuition can greatly affect the size of a TA's take-home pay.

Provides Teaching Experience

Teaching assistantships provide graduate students with valuable teaching experience. TAs usually have an opportunity to lead discussion and lab sections, lecture, advise students, grade papers, conduct review sessions, determine reading assignments, and design exams—all responsibilities the TA will have upon graduation to professordom.

A TAship is also a valuable employment credential for the graduate student. Most universities (and certainly all colleges) want evidence of teaching experience and ability prior to appointment. Candidates who were supported in graduate school by fellowhips and/or research assistantships alone (or who were not supported at all) may be considered suspect as teachers when seeking an initial tenure-track position. Ideally, a tenure-track appointee should provide evidence of both research and teaching competence.

Complements Graduate Education

Teaching assistantships afford graduate students an opportunity to learn their fields better, to review the basics of a field for subsequent comprehensive examinations, and to get a set of lecture notes for future professorial use. There is no way to internalize knowledge more effectively than by attempting to explain it to others. Michael J. Bozack, who has been a physics TA at Michigan State and at Carnegie-Mellon, advises TAs to "view recitation and lab as part of your preparation for qualifying exams." He observes that:

> It is common knowledge that a good way to start studying for masters qualifying exams is to do the hard problems in . . . texts. Learning is often enhanced when a person has to teach a discipline. I have found through teaching that concepts I thought I understood as an undergraduate were in actuality only crudely perceived. It is when one has to interact with questions and present material in a cohesive fashion that such incorrect notions can be identified and resolved. In short, rather than viewing recitation and lab as time lost to trivia, it is better to see them as contributing to your success as a graduate student.[30]

Further, a teaching assistantship may foster a close working relationship between a professor and a graduate student—clearly one of the goals of graduate education.

TAs personalize the undergraduate experience when they show concern for individual students.

Personalizes Undergraduate Education

For undergraduates, TAs can be an essential link in large, potentially impersonal universities. TAs often are agents of socialization, providing intellectual, emotional, and social support to freshmen and sophomores attempting to adjust to college. TAs are often the real "undergraduate advisers" in departments. Discussions sections, laboratories, and other small-group settings reduce the impersonality of the large university experience and make the facilitation of skill development in such areas as art, music, drama, speech communication, and physical education more feasible. Without TAs, undergraduates in large universities might do little more than attend large lecture classes taught by barely visible professors. TA-led sections may improve undergraduate morale and may allow instruction to take place at higher cognitive levels than is possible in lectures. TAs can explain confusing concepts and clarify abstract ideas. We have frequently overheard comments like, "Without the TA, I could never have made it through that class." As the Berkeley TA Training Project notes, "a TA-less Berkeley would be a nightmare for undergraduates, who would confront overcrowded seminars, inaccessible instructors and impersonal lectures."[31]

Uses Resources More Efficiently

The TA system enables an efficient use of human resources. By having graduate students teach lower-level courses and meet with small groups of students in discussion and laboratory sections, professors are freed to lecture to large groups of students and to teach upper-division and graduate-level courses. Through this system, professors who are excellent lecturers may be experienced by hundreds of students in large lecture halls with more personal, supportive instruction provided by TAs in discussion or laboratory section meetings. This system also enables professors to teach courses in their special areas of expertise to juniors, seniors, and graduate students.

Most TAs are happy to teach basic-level courses early in their graduate careers. As they grow in knowledge and teaching experience, graduate students are sometimes given the opportunity to teach middle-level, autonomous courses as lecturers.

Holds Social Advantages for TAs

A teaching assistantship is helpful socially. A TA is usually part of the "in" crowd among a department's graduate students. TAs have mailboxes and receive memos about department, college, and university happenings. TAs usually have offices—some of which serve as social centers as well as working areas. TAs are more likely to have occasion to talk with departmental secretaries and other supporting services employees than graduate students without an appointment.

A teaching assistantship may also aid a graduate student's social–emotional development. Standing in front of a class may help to develop self-assuredness. Student feedback and evaluations may provide the basis for TA growth and improvement. Positive TA–student interactions may provide the basis for lasting friendships.

Camaraderie often develops among TAs as a result of shared experiences.

In spite of the apparent benefits of the teaching assistant system, it is not without critics. Sykes alleges that TAs are simply "cheap labor" who are often as "confused as the students are."[32] While Sykes is often guilty of hyperbole, TAs do face a number of difficulties in carrying out their responsibilities. In this section three challenges will be considered.

Challenges Faced by Teaching Assistants

Lack of TA Training

It has been wryly noted that "college teaching is the only profession requiring no formal training of its practitioners."[33] In the mid-1960s, one critic, after studying university programs of teacher training, argued that universities have "thoroughly abused and prostituted the chief means of training prospective teachers—the teaching assistantship."[34] More recently, another critic observed that "the typical university's progress across the terrain of TA training and support has been glacial."[35]

Fortunately, the importance of TA training is receiving greater recognition. A national conference on the employment and education of teaching assistants was held at the Ohio State University in November of 1986.[36] An article in *The Chronicle of Higher Education* reported that many universities are now taking "extra steps to insure that graduate students know how to teach."[37] Among the extra steps that are being taken are the production of TA handbooks, the establishment of campus teaching centers and workshops, and the development of departmental workshops, short courses, and seminars in teaching. New TAs have a right to inquire about the availability of such services on their campuses. When such services are not available, TAs can petition the department chair for better TA training and, while waiting for a response to the petition, may form a TA support group to talk about teaching with invited guests (e.g., course directors and experienced TAs).

TA Personal Insecurity

Most new (and even experienced) TAs probably approach their responsibilities with a twinge of insecurity. The following fantasy is a far cry from reality:

> Twice a week you walk through the classroom door to be greeted by thirty upturned faces—there were twenty to start with, but your spreading renown has attracted others—and a clamor of questions about the week's lectures and the problem set. Suavely and with unfailing good humor you deal with these, providing the needed insight with a few deft words. Now and then you delve into your experience to provide the striking example which animates what had seemed to be just dead knowledge, or a lively anecdote which places the subject in a human context. If the week's lectures have been difficult, you may spend part of a period offering to your students your own view of the material: it is penetrating and clarifying, and your students interrupt you with perceptive questions and comments. Grading their problem sets and exams is a joy as you chart their steadily growing competence. They badger

you to find out what you are teaching next semester and what the best sequel to the course would be. No evaluation is needed: the glow in their eyes tells all.[38]

The appropriate rejoinder to this fantasy is "Earth to TA. Earth to TA." Unfortunately, there are several reasons why TAs may feel insecure.

Some TAs are insecure because of cultural or linguistic differences. While there appear to be no reliable surveys or estimates of the number of foreign TAs in American universities, their numbers are certainly substantial.[39] Many universities—some at the insistence of state legislatures—are now requiring that nonnative speakers take an oral proficiency exam to demonstrate English competence. Those who fail (but are academically eligible for financial assistance) may be awarded fellowships or given other nonteaching assignments the first semester or year. At the same time they may be required to audit the course they are likely to teach. They are also given a crash course(s) in English as a second language during that first semester or year. Such actions may not be enough, however. A 1979 survey of undergraduates at the University of Minnesota revealed that 43 percent felt that foreign TAs had harmed the course they had taken, while only 9 percent felt the course had been improved by the foreign TA.[40] A Cornell University report on the quality of undergraduate instruction admitted that students often complain about foreign TAs ("the University is so little concerned with our problems that it does not even take the trouble to ensure that all teaching assistants speak English well enough for us to understand").[41]

Another factor causing insecurity is inexperience, since many TAs are first-year graduate students who have never taught before. Being new to graduate school, often new to an institution, and sometimes relatively new to an academic field is not a prescription for competence and confidence. Still, many departments rely on first-year graduate students as TAs. First-semester TAs, besides lacking teaching experience, may also lack knowledge of campus geography, policies, and resources. New TAs need to learn about available services on campus for students (reading labs, writing labs, diagnostic services) and for TAs as well (manuals, TA classes, TA consultants, and educational service bureaus).

Graduate students may also be given assignments for which they are ill-prepared. For example, graduate students typically have sole responsibility for skill instruction in foreign languages. This practice is defended on the basis of economics, the desire of faculty to teach more advanced courses, and the belief that graduate students have the same qualifications as high school foreign language teachers (a B.A. with a major in the appropriate language). The only problem with this comparison is that high school foreign language teachers have also studied educational theory and have had supervised teaching experiences. Additionally, TAs may be asked to teach classes outside their areas of expertise. A specialist in social deviance may be asked to teach rural sociology, or a student of plant pathology may be needed to lead laboratory sections in genetics.

Since personal insecurity is a source of stress for TAs, all parties to a TA assignment should seek to reduce the causes of such insecurity. The TA should do all in his or her power to acquire language proficiency, teaching insights, or subject matter expertise. Departments should monitor appointments carefully, provide necessary training, use TAs in positions that maximize the probability for success, and provide adequate supervision. Colleges should provide encouragement for and central coordination of training programs and services for TAs. While it is unlikely that all TAs in a department will be perfectly suited to their duties, factors that contribute to personal insecurity for TAs should be a point of major concern for all involved.

Time / Role Conflicts

Graduate students appointed as TAs may be pleased with the money, prestige, teaching experience, and office space afforded by the appointment. Still, they also find that the appointment creates a conflict with the imperatives of academic survival. A graduate student in a Ph.D program faces a long and winding road, with such obstacles as classes, research seminars, master's papers, oral exams, and comprehensive qualifying exams—and then the dissertation (and trying to find a job). Graduate professors are not likely to accept deficient performance simply because the student was too busy with TA responsibilities to study properly.

Being a TA can be the downfall of a graduate student. Teaching assistants, especially those teaching for the first time, often find the experience exhilarating, particularly when compared with the potential drudgery of being in school for at least the seventeenth year. TAs are provided the emotional satisfaction of sharing their knowledge with others, of seeing their students grow intellectually, and of receiving positive feedback from their students. Such TAs may be tempted to devote the majority of their energies to teaching rather than to their own graduate work, thus running the risk of encountering that enemy of the successful graduate career—the incomplete.

Beginning TAs may find the time pressures of a teaching assistantship especially troublesome. Whereas TA reappointment often depends mainly on graduate school performance rather than on teaching performance, TAs may feel that they are being told, either implicitly or explicitly, that the TA responsibility comes ahead of graduate school courses.

TAs may also find their own graduate course selection impeded by a TA appointment. Lectures, labs, and discussion sections may be scheduled at the same time as classes a TA wishes to take. TAs are thus faced with the unpleasant choices of foregoing a desired graduate class, trying to get department officials to change the scheduled time of classes, or engaging a sympathetic professor or student to tape lectures.

TAs who are in the dissertation stage of their studies, and who no longer face the problem of incompletes, may find the temptation to devote excessive time to their students extremely acute since their time is more flexible after having completed classes and qualifying exams. Such TAs may also wind up as slaves to their students because such servitude is preferable to being a slave to the dissertation. A TAship can be fun; writing a dissertation can be a bear. Graduate professor David Sternberg reports that when he asks his students to word-associate to their dissertation, "some combination of the following responses is typical: fear, agony, torture, guilt, no end in sight, indefinitely postponed gratification, 'ruining my life, I'm drowning in it,' anxiety, boredom, hate, despair, depression, humiliation, powerlessness."[42]

Sternberg notes the growth of the ABD—the graduate student who has completed all requirements for the Ph.D. but the dissertation: "Each academic year throughout the 1980s more than 50,000 new ABDs will be generated by the American graduate school system. We will have over half a million ABDs during the decade."[43] Since completing a dissertation requires a Herculean effort, many candidates seem ill-matched to the challenge. Sternberg has noted that while 50,000 ABDs are created each year, only about 20,000 earned doctorates emerge each year.[44] The median time lapse from B.A. to Ph.D. for various fields is 6.8 years of "registered time" (the period of actual graduate school residence) and 10 years total time. The median age for new Ph.Ds is 33 years.[45]

While it is impossible to attribute the "Ph.D. stretchout" problem to TA responsibilities alone, Kenneth Wilson observed, in an early study of the length of doctoral programs, that "research appointments were infrequently evaluated as contributing to 'length,' whereas teaching assistantships were frequently judged to have had a lengthening influence."[46]

The message for the teaching assistant is clear: academic survival is paramount. Spending an excessive amount of time being a TA because of love for the activity is self-defeating, since a failed graduate career usually inhibits, if not prohibits, a TA from undertaking the activity permanently as a professor.

If a graduate student finds the TA appointment simply overwhelming in terms of its time requirements, perhaps the student should voluntarily decline reappointment. Short of this, TAs should bring to the attention of course directors assignments that require more hours than the number for which they are paid. In any event, TAs must recognize that their graduate school years require intense dedication and time management skills.

Summary

Many new graduate students are unfamiliar with the nature of teaching assistantships. Although the teaching assistantship system was rooted in the late nineteenth century, the full flowering of the system awaited the growth of the undergraduate population following World War II. Federal programs during the last three decades have contributed to a dramatic growth in the size of the TA population in American universities. At the present time, the generic term teaching assistant is used to refer to a variety of titles and teaching responsibilities. The benefits of this system are many. The teaching assistant system helps finance graduate education, provides teaching experience for future professors, complements graduate education, personalizes undergraduate education, uses university resources more efficiently, and holds social advantages for TAs. In spite of the benefits of the system, however, TAs face challenges posed by a lack of TA training, TA personal insecurity, and time/role conflicts.

Notes

1. Gene L. Woodruff, Dean of the Graduate School, "The Graduate Teaching Assistant" (videotape), University of Washington, Instructional Development and Research Center, 1985.
2. The history of the teaching assistantship prior to World War II is based on John L. Chase, *Graduate Teaching Assistants in American Universities: A Review of Recent Trends and Recommendations* (Washington, D.C.: U.S. Department of Health, Education, and Welfare, May 1970), pp. 3–4.
3. Richard J. Storr, *The Beginning of Graduate Education in America* (Chicago: University of Chicago Press, 1953), pp. 130–31.
4. W. Carton Ryan, *Studies in Early Graduate Education* (New York: Carnegie Foundation for the Advancement of Teaching, Bulletin No. 30, 1938), pp. 32, 33, 56, 120.
5. Richard R. Ely, *Ground Under Our Feet* (New York: Macmillan, 1938), p. 109.
6. Chase, p. 3.
7. Chase, p. 3.
8. William Lyon Phelps, *Teaching in School and College* (New York: Macmillan, 1912), pp. 119–20.
9. The Carnegie Foundation for the Advancement of Teaching, *The Control of the Campus: A Report on the Governance of Higher Education* (Princeton: Princeton University Press, 1982), p. 45.
10. Charles Kraus, "The Evolution of the American Graduate School," *AAUP Bulletin* 37:3 (Autumn 1951): 501–2.
11. Chase, p. 3.
12. Chase, p. 14.
13. Carnegie Foundation, p. 45
14. Carnegie Foundation, p. 45.

14

15. Leslie Maitland Werner, "Senate Extends Law Providing Student Loans," *New York Times*, June 4, 1986, p. 1.
16. Walter P. Metzger, "The American Academic Profession in 'Hard Times'," *Daedalus* 104:1 (Winter 1975): 37.
17. National Center for Education Statistics, *Digest of Education Statistics, 1983–84* (Washington, D.C.: United States Government Printing Office, December 1983), p. 101.
18. National Center, p. 103.
19. Chase, p. 2.
20. Richard A. Barella, *Graduate Service Assistants: A Research Report* (Muncie, Ind.: Ball State University, 1976), p. 1.
21. "Change Proposed in Graduate Student Teaching Titles," *Teaching at Berkeley* 18 (Fall 1985): 1.
22. Personal communication, David N. Redman, Assistant Dean, Princeton University, July 30, 1986.
23. *Handbook for TAs and AIs* (Austin, Tex.: University of Texas, 1982).
24. *The TA at UCLA* (Los Angeles: University of California at Los Angeles, 1984–1985), p. 6.
25. *The TA at UCLA*, p. 6.
26. "Report of the Committee on Teaching Assistants," University of Wisconsin–Madison, Faculty Document 477, April 4, 1982.
27. Leon D. Epstein, *Governing the University: The Campus and the Public Interest* (San Francisco: Jossey-Bass, 1974), pp. 28–29.
28. *Learning to Teach: A Handbook for Teaching Assistants at U.C. Berkeley* (Berkeley: The TA Training Project of the Graduate Assembly, 1985), Foreward, no page.
29. See for example, *TAs as Teachers: A Handbook for Teaching Assistants at UCSB* (Santa Barbara: University of California–Santa Barbara, 1984–85), p. 71; *The TA at UCLA*, p. 7; and The University of Texas at Austin, Office of the President, Policy Memorandum 8.101, "Rates of Pay and Notification of Proposed Employment for Teaching Assistants," September 1, 1986. Extensive surveys of TA pay are available from American Association of Universities, June 25, 1984, unpublished survey; and from the Office of the Dean for Graduate Studies, University of Nebraska–Lincoln, March 15, 1986.
30. Michael J. Bozack, "Tips for TA's: The Role of the Physics Teaching Assistant," *The Physics Teacher* 21: 1 (January 1983): 28.
31. *Learning to Teach*, p. 3.
32. Charles J. Sykes, *ProfScam: Professors and the Demise of Higher Education* (Washington, D.C.: Regnery Gateway, 1988), pp. 41, 43.
33. Vincent Nowlis, Kenneth E. Clark, and Miran Rock, *The Graduate Student as Teacher* (Washington, D.C.: American Council on Education, 1968), pp. iii.
34. W. Max Wise, "Who Teaches the Teachers?" in *Improving College Teaching: Aids and Impediments* Calvin T. B. Lee, ed. (Washington, D.C.: American Council on Education, 1966), pp. 90.
35. *How to Succeed as a New Teacher: A Handbook for Teaching Assistants* (New Rochelle, N.Y.: Change Magazine Press, 1978), p. 8.
36. For a report of this conference see Nancy Van Note Chism, general editor, *Institutional Responsibilities and Responses in the Employment and Education of Teaching Assistants: Readings from a National Conference* (Columbus, Ohio: Center for Teaching Excellence, The Ohio State University, 1987).

37. Liz McMillen, "Teaching Assistants Get Increased Training," *The Chronicle of Higher Education*, October 29, 1986, p. 9.
38. *The Torch or the Firehose? A Guide to Section Teaching* (Cambridge: Massachusetts Institute of Technology, 1981), p. 3.
39. "At the University of Miami, for example, thirty-three of the fifty-six teaching assistants in math, physics, and chemistry, and 60 percent of engineering TAs, came from other countries." "Let's Talk It Over: Foreign TAs, U.S. Students Fight Culture Shock," *Newsweek on Campus*, December 1985, p. 43.
40. Joseph Mestenhauser et al., *Report of a Special Course for Foreign Teaching Assistants to Improve Their Classroom Effectiveness* (Minneapolis: University of Minnesota, International Student Adviser's Office and Program in English as a Second Language, May 1980), p. 7.
41. Chase, p. 14.
42. David Sternberg, *How to Complete and Survive a Doctoral Dissertation* (New York: St. Martin's Press, 1981), p. 13.
43. Sternberg, p. 8.
44. Sternberg, p. 9.
45. National Academy of Sciences, *Summary Report, 1984, Doctorate Recipients from United States Universities* (Washington, D.C.: National Academy Press, 1986), p. 34.
46. Kenneth W. Wilson, *Of Time and the Doctorate: A Report of an Inquiry into the Duration of Doctoral Study* (Atlanta: Southern Regional Education Board, 1965), p. 48.

2

TA Roles and Styles

"Imagining their first time in front of a class conjures up some of the worst fantasies teachers ever indulge in. Some imagine being unable to find the room—even if they have gone there before to check it out—or being proved hopelessly stupid by the first question students ask or being unable to say anything at all. Even if all goes well, few come away from that initial exposure without having experienced a rapid pulse, sweaty palms, and a dry mouth."[1]

Michele Fisher
Teaching at Stanford

Even the most intelligent and competent people become anxious as they approach classrooms as first-time teachers. Some new teachers suffer from such afflictions as "a rapid pulse, sweaty palms, and a dry mouth."

Since most new TAs have never taken a course in teaching, it is no small wonder that many of them feel anxiety about their upcoming teaching assignments. This chapter begins by directly addressing such feelings of self-doubt. It then moves to a consideration of the various roles that are served by teaching assistants. It concludes with a discussion of common teaching styles demonstrated by TAs.

On Becoming an Authentic TA

The most difficult time for a teaching assistant is the two or three days preceding the first term of an appointment. Imagine that moment. You have been assigned an office and a desk. You have been given a class roster, a textbook, and other necessary materials. You have all of the trappings associated with being a TA, but you are plagued by nagging self-doubts. Deep inside, you know that you don't know anything about teaching and you wonder if you know enough about your discipline.

The behavior of your office mates exacerbates the problem. Experienced office mates exude confidence and poise. They boast enthusiastically about past successes as TAs. Even the other new TAs seem buoyant and optimistic. They sit at their desks browsing casually through assigned course materials, occasionally highlighting a phrase or two with their colored, felt-tipped pens. In the midst of such experience and control, your panic grows. You find yourself thinking, "What if someone finds out that I'm not a real teaching assistant? I'm only me!"

The task is to make the transition from being plain old you to being you, the competent teaching assistant. How is this done? Three approaches are possible.[2]

Role Playing TA

When placed in new situations, many people simply role play the person they *think* they are expected to be. They construct in their minds a model of the ideal TA. The ideal TA is efficient: I'll take attendance quickly and get right into the material. The ideal TA is friendly: I'll ask them about their weekends and praise them for their achievements. The ideal TA is intellectually rigorous: I'll ask them questions that call for more than simple recall responses. The ideal TA is helpful: I'll give them tips for understanding the professor, the textbook, and/or the lab manual.

In the beginning, all new TAs engage in a bit of acting as they "try on" teaching roles. As an entry-level strategy, role playing is a natural point of departure. Since you have been employed as a TA, you may as well try to act like one. The danger with this approach is that you may become so concerned with role playing that you never permit the authentic you to emerge. TAs who hide behind TA roles often force students to hide behind traditional student roles. When this happens, teaching assistants and their students interact in role-to-role relationships rather than as authentic human beings.

Another approach to being a TA is to deny the importance of roles. If you subscribe to this approach, you just show up at the first class meeting as your ordinary self. You tell the students your first name and inform them that you have been assigned as their TA even though you don't know anything about teaching. You inform them that you will all be learning together and that you hope they will come to discussion sections with topics they wish to talk about.

Just Being One's Self

This "what you see is what you get" approach to being a TA has some appeal. TAs who adopt this approach do not hide behind TA roles. They come to their classes as real human beings with all the potentialities and limitations of the human condition. They accept their students as people and don't force them to play stereotypic student roles. They do not claim to be all-knowing; they simply claim to be doing their best as imperfect human beings.

This approach to being a TA is not without its shortcomings. Students are paying tuition with the expectation that they will receive instruction from competent professionals. Most students are not interested in studying their TAs as exemplars of the human condition; rather, they will settle for acquiring knowledge and skills normally associated with the title of the course. Also, TAs are expected to provide leadership and direction. TAs who merely show up for class meetings as "people" will be perceived by their students as persons who are reneging on their responsibilities. Finally, TAs must recognize that they are expected to grade students. It is difficult to just be yourself when you have been empowered to and are expected to make positive and negative judgments about the persons with whom you are interacting. While it may seem honest and open to just be one's self as a TA, such an approach is probably not possible.

If one can't simply hide behind TA roles and can't just be one's self, what is a new TA to do? The process of becoming an authentic TA involves blending the dimensions of self with the roles of being a TA.

Responsible Role Taking

TAs come to the moment of truth with personalities that have been shaped by twenty-plus years of living. TAs are confident or shy, articulate or inarticulate, organized or disorganized. They must start with who they are.

In addition, TAs are expected to serve a myriad of roles (discussed in the next section) that help determine the range of appropriate behaviors. The task for TAs is to continually blend who they are with what they must do. For example, when leading a group discussion or when giving a lecture, the TA must be a bigger-than-life version of self. These particular roles require a public version of self that is more animated and dynamic and require considerably more energy than one's informal version of self. Initially, TAs who are unaccustomed to being public persons will have to role play being lecturer, discussion leader, or lab director. Eventually, as TAs grow into the variety of teaching duties, they find themselves feeling comfortable in a variety of contexts performing a variety of functions. They role play less and less as their personalities take on or accommodate teaching roles.

The path to becoming an effective TA is not a straight line. It meanders a good bit and it is punctuated by false starts and even major reversals. But in the long run, the goal is to develop a teaching style that is both comfortable and effective. Some specimen teaching styles are considered in the third section of this chapter.

Teaching Assistant Roles

Teaching assistants are expected to perform a number of roles. In this section, consideration will be given to four different categories of roles: instructional, interactive, administrative, and institutional. This discussion of roles is included here as an overview. Many of these roles will receive detailed treatment in subsequent chapters.

Instructional Roles

Instructional roles refer to duties that involve direct interaction with students in classroom settings. All TAs are expected to present information, to make assignments, to review content, to lead discussions, to oversee small-group work, to supervise laboratories, to ask questions, and to proctor examinations. Each of these instructional roles should be approached in a self-reflective manner.

Interactive Roles

Interactive roles refer to duties that involve interactions with students in nonclassroom settings. Students often ask TAs to *provide feedback*. One of the main reasons for establishing office hours is to provide an opportunity for students to discuss their progress on a project, paper, or speech. They want a caring TA to look at their work and to provide an intelligent response. In providing feedback, TAs must make evaluative judgments about the work and report those judgments in an elaborated manner.

Students also expect TAs to *give advice*. In addition to providing feedback, students expect TAs to provide helpful advice about their work: What changes should be made? What additional sources should be consulted? What work strategies might prove to be the most productive? At times it is totally appropriate for TAs to answer such questions directly. On other occasions, in order to stimulate student thinking, such questions may be best answered with other questions.

When students experience problems, they often expect their TA to *act as a counselor*. In this role, the TA tries to help students work their way through a personal or academic problem by asking open-ended questions designed to help them clarify their thoughts and identify alternative solutions to their problems. The final choice of a solution must, of course, rest with the student. The TA as counselor must also know his or her limitations. Some students have very serious problems that a TA cannot resolve through amateur therapy. In these cases, students should be referred to appropriate campus agencies for professional assistance.

When students stop by during office hours, they expect the TA to *function as a tutor*. Tutoring involves an interactive exchange, the nature of which is determined by the learning task. In some cases tutoring involves providing examples, definitions, descriptions, or restatements of the concept or phenomenon in question. In other cases tutoring involves asking process questions as students work their way through problems or seek to understand events.

Administrative roles refer to duties that relate to the instructional process but that are not instructive in their own right. All TAs must *make plans*. The planning role is absolutely essential to effective teaching. Planning involves a variety of activities including writing objectives, identifying content, preparing handouts, devising learning activities, and phrasing questions.

TAs are often expected to *take attendance*. While taking attendance in discussion or laboratory sections is easily accomplished, doing so in a huge lecture hall may be a challenging though necessary task. For example, in one course in a midwestern university, students are given credit for attending concerts of visiting musical groups. Taking attendance ensures that visiting groups will have a suitable audience. The class, popularly called "clap for credit," does expose students to a variety of musical forms. But think of the poor TA diligently trying to discover who is missing from seat G in row forty-seven. Try though they may, it is not likely that TAs can find a creative or efficient way of taking mass attendance.

Administrative Roles

TAs must frequently *prepare tests* and other means of assessment. While not all TAs are expected to construct tests, many are. The ability to design valid and reliable tests is an important ingredient in effective teaching. To do so, TAs must sample from all areas covered in lectures or reading assignments, must understand the potentialities and limitations of various kinds of test items, must prepare questions that are clear and unambiguous, and must have an intuitive sense of which questions will work.

Nearly all TAs can expect to *grade student work*. Since grading can be a long and tedious process, requiring both intelligence and sound judgment, it is often an exhausting business. As a general policy, grading should be completed as soon after the work is submitted as possible. Students are highly intolerant of TAs who do not return work promptly.

TAs assigned to lecture courses are sometimes expected to *provide instructional media services*. Since such courses sometimes meet in halls that have the capability for multimedia instruction, TAs so assigned must become familiar with the wide array of equipment that may be used to complement the professor's lectures. Since equipment malfunction can ruin a lecture, it is necessary for these TAs to become highly proficient in the use of film projectors, slide projectors, overhead projectors, various VCR formats, and the like. The best way to become familiar with such equipment is to use it, over and over again, in the presence of a competent technician. TAs in such courses may also be called upon to lug equipment across campus, to create slides or videotapes, and to search for media software in catalogues. TAs may also use instructional media in teaching their own autonomous sections.

The final administrative task is to *keep records*. Some departments issue grade books to TAs and expect attendance, grades, and other information to be dutifully recorded in a precise and systematic matter. In other cases, TAs are expected to devise their own systems. It is important that a TA have a system for recording information. It is also important that a TA have a system for translating that information into a final grade, instead of merely "eyeballing" the line of grades for each student and concluding, "It looks like a C to me." The determination of final grades should involve mathematical precision rather than casual estimation.

Institutional Roles

Institutional roles have very little, if anything, to do with teaching. They are largely defined by the rules and customs of individual institutions.

A very important institutional role is to *be an office mate*. In many cases, the primary criterion used in assigning TAs to offices is smoking preference. This is, of course, an important criterion since TA offices are often overcrowded, windowless, and improperly ventilated. Other than smoking, social mores regarding being a good office mate are determined by informal consensus in each office. Since expectations are not codified, it is necessary to figure out the nature of the consensus. In one office, TAs have acquired the habit over the years of not turning on the overhead fluorescent lights. Rather, all TAs supply table lamps for their desks. Each year, as new TAs join experienced TAs in the office, they can be seen within the first several days carrying table lamps into the building.

Common sense can help a great deal in establishing and maintaining harmonious office relationships. For example, it is helpful if office mates schedule office hours at different times to minimize the noise and confusion in any one time slot. When a TA is talking with a student, office mates should not interrupt to correct, extend, or make humorous remarks. Office mates should take turns answering the phone and responding to students who appear at the door. Finally, they should never talk in disparaging terms about an office mate when speaking with that TA's students.

When office mates learn to live in harmony, they can be of great value to each other. They can share teaching tips and information about professors, the department, and the academic discipline. They can provide emotional support in times of stress and camaraderie in happy moments. They might even be able to cover for each other in times of illness.

Another important role is to *be a member of a course staff.* In some cases a single TA is assigned to work under the direction of a professor. In other cases, however, a number of TAs are assigned to a course to work under the direction of a professor. When this happens, TAs must be concerned about their relationships with a course staff consisting of peers as well as the professor. Peers become upset with fellow TAs who fail to do their fair share of the work, who blatantly curry the favor of the professor, or who are inflexible in staff planning meetings. When serving on a course staff, TAs are well advised to be team players.

A final institutional role is to *be a citizen* of the university. Departments have expectations, written and unwritten, about such things as keeping office hours, reporting enrollments, using the copy machine, sharing and caring for a mailbox, signing up for videotape equipment, rearranging classroom furniture, turning out lights, attending staff meetings, and reacting to a myriad of other nondiscretionary happenstances.

A citizen is also governed by rules and procedures at the college and university levels. Colleges have rules about such things as not teaching at all if one has fellowship support, being evaluated by students and the course supervisor, holding class in the assigned room, responding to student dishonesty, and giving permission for students to be used as subjects in research projects. Universities have regulations about getting final grades in promptly, posting grades by ID number rather than name, not

Multi-section courses often call for staff planning sessions.

engaging in sexual harrassment, not smoking in class, and not parking one's bicycle inside classroom buildings. While some rules and regulations deserve to be challenged, TAs as citizens must weigh the consequences of dissent and must select appropriate means of redressing grievances.

Teaching Assistant Styles

While there are many roles that teaching assistants must assume, there are also various styles that they may adopt as they assume their responsibilities. Style refers to the TA's modus operandi. It is important that TAs be aware of alternative styles that are available to them. Then, they must try out these styles until they find one that suits them well. There is a problem, however. Most of the literature on styles refers either to school teacher styles or professorial styles. As an example of the latter, Adelson, using a religious analogy, classifies professors under three headings: *shamans,* who gather student disciples around them to bask in the warmth of their wisdom; *priests,* who focus their students' attention on their subject matter and who are faithful to their disciplines; and *mystic healers*, who are primarily concerned about students and their welfare and development.[3]

It should be apparent, however, that this system, although intriguing as a means of categorizing professors, doesn't work well for TAs. TAs lack the status and longevity of *shamans*. Indeed, without the doctoral collar, they even lack credibility as *priests*. Thus, the system leaves only the style of the *mystic healer*. While this style is not inappropriate for TAs, the categorical system, stripped of its shamans and priests, is lacking in theoretical richness.

Systems for classifying TA styles are less global in nature since they tend to be tied to TAs in particular subject matter fields or to other special subsets of the TA population. For example, TA styles in one English department manual are labeled authority figure, lecturer, Socratic questioner, workshop leader, moderator, and literature and writing aficionado.[4] Another system, used in categorizing foreign TAs, includes five classes: active unintelligibles, mechanical problem solvers, knowledgeable helpers/casual friends, entertaining allies, and inspiring cheerleaders.[5]

This section identifies a different system for categorizing TA styles. It is hoped that the five negative and five positive styles will be useful to TAs as they ponder their own teaching styles.

TAs who have an ineffective teaching style are often unaware of the impression they give to their students. First-term TAs are frequently shocked by end-of-course student evaluations. They had assumed that all was well with their teaching and that their students both liked and respected them. Among the styles that students do not like or respect are the five that follow.

Negative Teaching Assistant Styles

The Bore   In the classroom of the boring TA, the most interested and active person present is the instructor, who talks on and on about the facts, concepts, laws, or precepts that illumine the discipline. Since the instructor is doing all, or almost all, of the talking, the class period passes rapidly for him or her; however, the same instructional period may seem incredibly long and boring for the students. Few students have a forty-five- to fifty-minute attention span. Few lecturers are sufficiently dynamic, creative, and entertaining that student attention may be sustained for such a period of time. What TAs must understand is that most undergraduate students do not share their love for the discipline. The bore merely presents the material to students; no attempt is made to relate the information to student needs and interests. In turn, the students doze, doodle, and daydream. But, being enamored of his or her own voice, the bore never notices.

The Boor   A boor is a person who is lacking in the social graces. TAs who are boors treat their students in a rude, cool, or distant manner. They belittle student questions; they interrupt student responses; they show little respect for student ability; they smirk instead of smile. The most offensive of boors are TAs who are arrogant about their own intellectual achievements. They treat students with great disdain since they

consider the undergraduate mind incapable of the high level of intellectual exchange the TA values. Not all TAs who are perceived as boors
are arrogant, however. In many cases, TAs who are shy or apprehensive
try to conceal their uncertainty by showing little of their personalities
to students. In the process they seem overbearing, haughty, and distant.
They communicate to students that they do not wish to establish cordial
interpersonal relationships. While students could have accepted their
shyness, their boorish cover-up is totally unacceptable.

The Flake   The flake suffers from terminal disorganization. TAs who
are flakes have difficulty getting to class on time. Once they get there,
it takes them a long time to get everything sorted out. Discussion notes
fall to the floor. Needed instructional supplements are not in their back-
packs or briefcases. Tests the students expected back are on the TA's
desk in an office four buildings away. That desk reflects the personality
of its absent user: layers of clutter everywhere, nary a spot available for
honest pen and paper work, a half-eaten apple in the outbasket. It doesn't
take long for students to recognize that a TA is a flake. In addition to
looking flakey, the flake is intellectually disorganized. Assignments are
made in a haphazard manner. Class discussions seem to wander. Information is not presented in a clear and straightforward manner.

The Fake   TAs are sometimes assigned to teach or assist in courses
outside their areas of primary expertise. When this happens, it is expected that they will expend considerable energy in mastering the subject matter before attempting to teach it to others. Some TAs, however,
decide to take a shortcut through the preparatory process by keeping a
few pages ahead of the students and by "winging it" in class discussions.
The fake doesn't succeed. When a TA doesn't know the material, students can tell: factual errors are made, questions are avoided or answered in an evasive manner, information is presented in a hesitant or
halting fashion. There is no substitute for knowing the material. To accept
a teaching assistantship is to take on the obligation of becoming appropriately informed.

The Wimp   A wimp is a wishy-washy person. TAs who are wimps are
highly uncertain about matters of pedagogy. They make assignments in
a tentative manner; in fact, assignments often sound more like questions
than statements. Wimps refuse to accept responsibility for the courses
they teach. When students complain about course content, procedures,
or expectations, the wimp is likely to say, "I don't like it either, but that's
the way Professor Smedley wants it done." Undergraduates soon learn
that a wimpy TA is a person to be manipulated rather than respected.
They maneuver the wimp into modifying assignments, changing due

dates, and wasting class time justifying course content and procedures. TAs who are wimps use the words "I'm caught in the middle" with great frequency, but no one believes them.

Effective teaching assistants can employ vastly differing teaching styles. In this section five positive teaching styles will be discussed.

Positive Teaching Assistant Styles

The Brilliant Eccentric   Certain TAs are effective because their exceptional intellects command the attention and respect of their students. Such TAs have excellent verbal fluency and adorn their ideas in vivid language that is skillfully spoken. They are often a bit unorthodox in appearance and behavior. Because of their dedication to matters of the mind, they may give little attention to dress and personal grooming. They develop mannerisms that set them aside from others; they may pace back and forth as they speak or they may lead a class discussion while sitting cross-legged, guru style, on their desks. But it really doesn't matter. Students like and respect brilliant eccentric teaching assistants. They wouldn't change them if they could.

The Entertainer   Other TAs are successful because they are entertaining. They are gifted storytellers and they use language in creative and humorous ways. They dominate the classroom because they like to be the center of attention. But their students don't notice. They refer to their students by name often and build illustrative materials out of the lives of their students. Entertainers take a personal interest in their students because they want to adapt their "material" to their audience's interests, needs, and senses of humor.

The Basic Competent   Some TAs are effective because they have basic teaching competence. They don't display their intelligence as do brilliant eccentrics and flashy entertainers; still, they get the job done. Basic competents are the reverse of flakes. They have clear goals in mind. They communicate their expectations to students in clear assignments. They set and adhere to deadlines. They grade and return work promptly. They are efficient in leading class discussions. When presenting information they are clear and straightforward. They are never tardy. They are always in their offices during announced office hours. They are dependable.

The Helpmate   The helpmate style places high time demands on TAs. Helpmates go out of their way to ensure that their students will do well: they hold extra office hours before major assignments are due, they hold evening review sessions before tests, they invite students to call them at home with questions, they convey student concerns to the professor, they call students who have been absent twice in a row to find out if they are ill. Helpmates are basically nice people who treat their students with affection and respect and who are, in turn, liked and respected by their students.

The Mentor   The mentor is a wise and trustworthy person who takes a personal interest in the intellectual development of his or her students. Mentors teach by example as well as by precept. They have exceptionally high standards of scholarship; they demand a great deal of themselves and, consequently, expect a great deal of their students. Mentors serve as role models of the skills and habits of inquiry they seek to impart. In laboratory sections, TA mentors perform as scientists who wish their students to join the investigative team. In discussion sections, mentors ask questions of the sort that are examined by scholars in the discipline. Mentors, in sum, are dedicated to both scholarship and teaching.

While this system for categorizing teaching assistant styles is stereotypical, it does represent the range of styles one finds among TAs in a large department. TAs may, of course, possess characteristics from two or more of these categories. The important point is that TAs need not be locked hopelessly into negative styles. TAs can change and grow as they acquire experience. Before such growth can occur, however, TAs must be sensitive to the image they project to their students. TAs are not likely to change if they deceive themselves about their popularity and effectiveness.

TAs in Terra Incognita

All new TAs fret about assuming teaching duties. All new TAs must assume a myriad of roles and must try on teaching styles to use in accomplishing such roles. All TAs, however, do not face equal challenges.

In addition to the normal challenges, some TAs take on the added burden of having to adjust to terra incognita—an unknown land. Major research universities attract graduate students from all parts of the nation and the world. Many of these graduate students, at one time or another, enter undergraduate classrooms as teaching assistants. For example, at the University of California, Berkeley, 13 percent of the TAs "are from non–English speaking countries."[6] In mathematics, one-third of TAs in universities across the nation are foreign-born.[7] The use of teaching assistants from distant lands and cultures poses two kinds of problems: linguistic problems and problems caused by cultural disparity.

While foreign students enrich campus life and are often exceptionally able scholars, their appointment as teaching assistants can be problematic if they have not mastered the English language. For example, one undergraduate student dropped out of an electrical engineering program when he was assigned, for the third semester in a row, to a discussion section taught by a foreign graduate student. In another case, a foreign graduate student sought help in the English language after she had been "teaching" for a full semester. Her English skills were so impoverished that it was necessary for her to repeat the title of her major, meteorology, five times before anyone on the screening panel could understand her. The national scope of the problem was attested to by the December 1985 issue of *Newsweek on Campus* which concluded, after surveying the use of TAs across a number of campuses nationally, that "some TAs speak in broken English" while "some barely speak at all."[8]

The problem is most acute in fields such as computer science, engineering, mathematics, and the sciences.[9] In these fields, foreign students compete very favorably with American students for graduate admission because of the excellence of their previous training in mathematics and the sciences. Since American students in these areas are often lured away from academe by higher salaries in business and industry,[10] departments may feel compelled to use foreign TAs who are marginally competent in the English language in order to staff necessary courses.

Increasingly, American institutions are requiring that foreign graduate students demonstrate English language competence before they are offered teaching assistantships. Most universities now require that foreign graduate students take the Test of English as a Foreign Language (TOEFL).[11] "This test, which has been shown to be valid and reliable when used for its intended purpose, measures the ability to understand spoken and written English in an academic context."[12] Students who score well on this written test, however, may still have difficulty communicating orally with American students who are unaccustomed to speaking with people who have foreign accents. Consequently, many universities are demanding additional proof of English language competence. Some universities require that prospective foreign TAs take a test of spoken English (TSE) as a complement to TOEFL.[13] Other schools require that foreign graduate students support themselves during their first year on campus while an assessment of their competence is made as they interact with American speakers of the English language. Whatever the system employed, American universities must ensure that potential teaching assistants have demonstrated English language competence before they are appointed as teaching assistants.

Once foreign graduate students are appointed as TAs, it becomes their responsibility to continue to grow in communication competence in the English language. Jia-Yush Yen, a University of California, Berkeley, TA in mechanical engineering from Taiwan, urges foreign TAs to speak in English as often as they can, to listen closely to radio and television, to read aloud to sharpen pronunciation, and to learn to think in English.[14] Dong-Gyom Kim, a Berkeley TA in mathematics from South Korea, agrees about the usefulness of watching television, "even 'Sesame Street' and 'Bugs Bunny' cartoons," and also emphasizes the importance of imitation, practice, and singing English songs.[15] In addition to these suggestions, foreign TAs may use facial expressions and gestures to complement their verbal messages and may use visual aids and chalkboard notations to visually represent their oral presentations.

Cultural Disparity

To an extent, all graduate students who venture forth from their undergraduate colleges or universities to different institutions for graduate study are moving to terra incognita. Given proficiency in the English language, the move from a Japanese university to an American university is different only in degree from a move from Queens College in New York City to a midwestern or western university. In fact, some undergraduate students have alleged that the TAs who are the most difficult to understand and relate to come from New York City rather than from Tokyo, Paris, Lagos, or Brasilia.[16]

American TAs who are younger than or older than the norm also suffer from cultural disparity. Gifted students sometimes begin graduate study when they are between sixteen and twenty years of age. When such "youngsters" are appointed as teaching assistants, they run the risk of being perceived as whippersnappers by their older, if not wiser, students. Similarly, older TAs may be perceived by their students as anachronisms—creatures lingering far after their proper historical time.

Whatever the cause of the cultural disparity, TAs so afflicted must do their best to cope with the special circumstances surrounding their employment. The guidelines that follow suggest coping mechanisms.

Capitalize on the Cause of the Disparity TAs who are younger than or considerably older than their students, or who differ from their students racially or culturally, should perceive such differences as a potential teaching asset rather than as a teaching liability. TAs representing different cultures, races, or ages can increase the interest levels of their teaching if they are willing to disclose information about their families, backgrounds, and native cultures. Such information often can be blended with subject matter as examples of concepts.

TAs from other countries can draw on their own cultures to enrich classroom discussions.

Modify Expectations   Gary Althen, in his *Manual for Foreign Teaching Assistants* at the University of Iowa, has observed that "most foreign TAs are suprised at the *low level of academic preparation* of some of their United States students, especially the freshmen."[17] In many countries, only the most gifted students are permitted to attend college. Foreign TAs who come from such countries expect to find in freshman classes the crème de la crème. Similarly, TAs from disadvantaged minorities and TAs who are unusually young expect from students the same high level of dedication and performance that characterized their own work. Older TAs expect their students to behave as they think they behaved in a time obscured by the passage of years. In each of these scenarios, TAs are well advised to accept their students as they are. TAs who are disappointed with the intellectual acuity of their students are unlikely to treat their students with respect. In return, such TAs are unlikely to receive the affection and respect of their students.

Do Not Take Offense Where No Offense Is Intended   Contemporary undergraduate students in the United States have been characterized as being "informal."[18] It is true that young people in the United States are less gifted in social amenities than students in some other cultures. American students often address TAs by their first names, put feet on furniture, challenge the accuracy of information presented by TAs, eat and drink in the classroom, and quibble over evaluations made by TAs. While such student behaviors might seem unusually offensive in other cultures, in the United States students normally behave in these ways without meaning to offend their instructors. Students in American universities "tease" teaching assistants whom they are fond of and respect. It is easy for foreign TAs to take the content of such taunts literally. It is a great mistake to do so. Teasing is often a sign of affection rather than contempt or lack of respect in the American culture.

Strive for Clarity   American students are not known for their tolerance of accents. Midwestern undergraduate students often criticize TAs from the eastern states for saying "idear," "strenth," "tornament," and the like. Midwestern TAs teaching in the south have been told that they talk too fast or that their voices are too nasal. American undergraduate students seem to go out of their way to be bothered by foreign accents. Students grouse about being in discussion sections with foreign TAs even when the English of the foreign TA is of better quality than the language of the students in the class.

Recognizing this intolerance, TAs who differ from their students should, above all else, strive for clarity. Assignments should be written on the chalkboard as well as presented orally. Handouts should be used liberally to support oral presentations. The speaking rate should be reduced if necessary. Key phrases should be repeated to facilitate student note-taking. Gestures and facial expression should be used to help clarify language meaning. Student feedback should be invited with frequency. TAs who do these things will discover that student intolerance soon dissipates.

Be Friendly   Gary Althen has observed that although American undergraduates "do not *demand* friendliness and openness . . . they *like* it and usually respond positively toward it. They are likely to work harder for a teacher whom they like than for one whom they do not like."[19] While visiting the classroom of a foreign TA, one of the authors was approached by a student who observed, "We really like her. She is such a friendly and caring person. Working with her has been a very pleasant experience."

While teachers in some foreign cultures are afforded high status and are expected to act in an aloof and dignified manner, in the United States TAs who act in this manner will be considered boors and will be disliked by their students. Students who receive positive expressions of affect from their TAs are likely to respond in kind, both on a daily basis and on end-of-term course evaluations.

Be Especially Helpful   Recognizing that linquistic problems and cultural disparity may make learning more difficult for their students, TAs should do their best to be especially helpful. Extra office hours will enable students who are experiencing difficulty to seek help in a nonthreatening environment. Time spent in one-to-one communication with students will benefit the TA as well by continuing to strengthen language skills. Before examinations, TAs can hold review sessions to ensure that students have a sound grasp of essential facts and concepts. Finally, such TAs can spend extra time evaluating and commenting on student homework and other written assignments.

Foreign TAs who solve their linguistic problems and who adapt to cultural disparity can perform with excellence in American college classrooms. Fortunately, an increasing number of departments are helping foreign TAs to do so by offering instruction in the English language and in pedagogy. *Newsweek on Campus* noted that "because of the attention paid to their teaching, some foreign TAs have become plainly better teachers than their American counterparts."[20]

Summary

New teaching assistants often experience anxiety as they are about to assume the duties of their positions. Three approaches to becoming an authentic TA are available: role playing being a TA, just being one's self, and responsible role taking. Among the roles that teaching assistants are expected to perform are: instructional roles such as presenting information, making assignments, reviewing content, asking questions, and proctoring examinations; interactive roles such as providing feedback, giving advice, acting as a counselor, and functioning as a tutor; administrative roles such as making plans, taking attendance, preparing tests, grading student work, providing instructional media services, and keeping records; and institutional roles such as being an office mate, being a member of a course staff, and being a citizen of the department, college, and university. In meeting the requirements of these roles, TAs can adopt a variety of styles. Among the negative styles that TAs inadvertently assume are the bore, the boor, the flake, the fake, and the wimp. Among the positive TA styles are the brilliant eccentric, the entertainer, the basic competent, the helpmate, and the mentor. TAs in terra incognita face two kinds of special challenges: linguistic problems and cultural disparity. University officials must ensure that foreign TAs are competent in the English language before they are appointed as TAs. Given competence in the English language, TAs may reduce cultural disparity by capitalizing on the source of the disparity, by modifying their expectations, by not taking offense where no offense is intended, by striving for clarity, by being friendly, and by being especially helpful.

Notes

1. Michele Fisher, ed., *Teaching at Stanford: An Introductory Handbook*, rev. ed. (Stanford, Calif.: Center for Teaching and Learning, Stanford University, 1983), p. 8.
2. These three approaches to assuming teaching roles are based on a conceptualization by Jo Sprague, "Approaching the Teacher Role," in R. R. Allen, S. Clay Willmington, and Jo Sprague, *Speech Communication in the Secondary School,* 2d ed. (Boston: Allyn and Bacon, 1976), pp. 156–62.
3. Joseph Adelson, "The Teacher as a Model," *The American Scholar* 30:3 (Summer 1961): 395–400. A more limited typology of professorial styles was advanced by Joseph Axelrod, *The University Teacher as Artist* (San Francisco: Jossey-Bass, 1973), p. 7. In this system, humanities professors are perceived as midwives (persons who help give "birth to ideas"), Jehovahs (God-like creatures who breath life into dust clods—college freshmen), and sowers of seeds (persons who sprinkle ideas on soil—both fertile and barren).
4. Richard Knowles, Beth Black, Jim Dersnah, Cherie Frascona, and Marilyn Reizbaum, *Handbook for Teaching Assistants in the English Department* (Madison: Department of English, University of Wisconsin–Madison, 1984), p. 18.
5. Kathleen M. Bailey, "A Typology of Teaching Assistants," in *Foreign Teaching Assistants in U.S. Universities,* eds. Kathleen M. Bailey, Frank Pialorsi, and Jean Zukowski/Faust (Washington, D.C.: National Association for Foreign Student Affairs, 1984), pp. 110–25.
6. Robby Cohen and Ron Robin, eds., *Teaching at Berkeley: A Guide for Foreign Teaching Assistants* (Berkeley: University of California, Berkeley, 1985), p. 7.
7. Scott Heller, "Problems Arise in Foreign-Student Programs," *The Chronicle of Higher Education*, October 29, 1986, p. 9.
8. "Lets Talk It Over: Foreign TAs, U.S. Students Fight Culture Shock," *Newsweek on Campus*, December 1985, p. 43.
9. Scott Heller, "Colleges Try Tests and Training to Make Sure Foreign TAs Can Be Understood," *The Chronicle of Higher Education,* September 11, 1985, p. 1.
10. *Newsweek on Campus,* p. 43.
11. Heller, p. 32.
12. Charles W. Stansfield and Rodney J. Ballard, "Two Instruments for Assessing the Oral Communication Proficiency of Foreign Teaching Assistants," in Bailey, et al., p. 101.
13. Bailey et al., pp. 101–8.
14. Jia-Yush Yen, "Overcoming the Language Barrier," in Cohen and Robin, pp. 17–18.
15. Dong-Gyom Kim, "Listening Comprehension and Accent Problems," in Cohen and Robin, pp. 22–25.
16. *Newsweek on Campus,* p. 43.
17. Gary Althen, *Manual for Foreign Teaching Assistants* (Iowa City: University of Iowa, 1981), p. 3.
18. Althen, p. 6.
19. Althen, p. 10.
20. *Newsweek on Campus,* p. 43.

3

Interpersonal Relationships

"For many students, you will be one of the first personal contacts they have in what can be a very intimidating environment. Some students will feel more comfortable talking with their teaching assistant than with their professors or other university staff members, and students may often turn to you for advice on both academic and nonacademic concerns. . . .

The relationship between the supervising faculty member and the teaching assistant is an important one for both, and you will find faculty members eager to work with you to ensure that students learn well and that the teachers of the course, the faculty member and the assistant, teach well. . . .

To be able to work cooperatively and effectively with departmental secretaries, lab personnel, and academic staff members will be a great asset and a significant help for you, both as you begin your teaching career and as you continue it."[1]

Manual for Teaching Assistants
University of Wisconsin

As this opening quotation reveals, teaching assistants are expected to establish and maintain harmonious relationships with a variety of people. To be effective in interpersonal relationships, TAs must be sensitive to the expectations and needs of others and respond appropriately.

This chapter begins by considering the types of students with whom a TA must relate. Some general guidelines for healthy TA–student relationships are then considered, followed by a discussion of the TA–professor relationship. The chapter concludes with a brief examination of TA relationships with members of the support staff.

Relating to Students of Varying Personalities

Being effective as a TA demands the ability to relate to a variety of students. Especially at large state universities, the undergraduate student body is likely to be extremely diverse, representing differing ages, intellectual abilities, and academic interests. Students will also vary greatly in emotional maturity and in their abilities to adapt to the social and intellectual demands of university life. Many students, especially first-semester freshmen, are intimidated by college. They are often surprised at the amount of work required and they are anxious about their ability to succeed—both academically and socially. TAs need to deal effectively with different types of students, including those described below.[2]

The Self-motivated Learner

Self-motivated learners, more likely to be found among juniors and seniors, have been weaned from the professor's spoon and are able to formulate their own educational objectives. Most self-motivated students are able to think creatively, participate in class easily, and feel comfortable socially with instructors. The literature on student learning styles refers to these students as "independent"[3] or "independent prone."[4] Such students prefer independent study, self-paced instruction, problems requiring independent thought, self-designed projects, and student-centered classroom settings.[5]

Self-motivated students, while not in need of day-to-day attention, do require an intelligent and caring mentor to ask questions and to provide encouragement. On occasion the TA as mentor can save self-motivated students from chasing the wild goose by pointing out likely avenues of inquiry.

The Respectful Learner

Respectful learners enjoy taking college courses and have great respect for their professors and TAs. They ask good questions in class and often seek out the TA or the professor for additional information. They are innately excited about learning and pursue new knowledge with vigor. In the learning styles literature, such students have been dubbed "participants"—people who want to learn course content, enjoy going to class, and thrive on class-related activities.[6] Respectful learners are a joy for the TA to behold. They can be counted on to be eager participants in class discussions and to be leaders in small-group activities.

The Submissive Student

Submissive students expect the professor or TA to tell them what to do. They expect to come to class, to sit quietly, and to take extensive notes. They neither expect nor desire to interact directly with the instructor. The Grasha–Riechmann student learning style typology identifies these students as "dependent" and provides the following description:

> This style is characteristic of students who show little intellectual curiosity and who learn only what is required. They see teacher and peers as sources of structure and support. They look to authority figures for guidelines and want to be told what to do.[7]

While some instructors may welcome a classroom full of submissive students, taken to an extreme this type of student offers little intellectual or emotional satisfaction for TAs. In fact, they may cause immense frustration to college teachers, as G. B. Trudeau's "Doonesbury" cartoon so vividly illustrates in figure 3.1. And of course, Doonesbury's professor was right: submissive students must be cajoled, challenged, and confronted. Alternative explanations of phenomena may be presented, requiring students to draw their own conclusions. Course objectives and tests can stress student thinking rather than just student recall or comprehension of facts. The TA can serve as the devil's advocate to challenge concepts commonly thought to be true. Whatever the method used, TAs need to encourage submissive students to present their own views rather than simply regurgitate the ideas presented to them.

The Paranoid Student

Paranoid students are like submissive students in that they want to be spoon-fed. The main difference is that they are afraid they will miss the feeding. Paranoid students live in the fear that they will miss something, and therefore constantly ask the instructor to repeat definitions and concepts. Paranoid students frequently are competitive and exhibit high ambition, anxiety, and suspicion. In the student learning styles literature, these students are referred to as "competitive." They vie with other students for grades and the teacher's attention and praise.[8]

It is easy for TAs to become irritated with paranoid students since they interrupt the instructional flow to request that information be repeated or more fully elaborated. Paranoids also seem to imply that the TA is out to get them by being vague or that the TA intends to be picky by testing for trivial information. In dealing with paranoid students, TAs should assure them that tests will involve major concepts and will be fair.

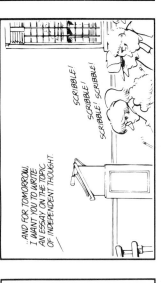

Figure 3.1
DOONESBURY COPYRIGHT 1985 G. B. Trudeau. Reprinted with permission of Universal Press Syndicate. All rights reserved.

Sample questions from previous tests may even be distributed to all class members to assure the paranoid that all is well. Having done this, the TA should ask the persistent paranoid to stop by after class so that his or her questions may be answered without taking class time to do so. Since the paranoid student thrives on praise, TAs may wish to provide some when it is deserved.

President Calvin Coolidge was the strong, silent type. A Washington society reporter, famed for her ability to make people talk, told Coolidge that she had bet a friend that she could elicit more than two words from him. Coolidge's response? "You lose."

The Calvin Coolidge Type

Many undergraduates are the silent type. Fearful of saying something stupid, they choose instead to remain silent. TAs should not ignore or give up on Calvin Coolidge types but should instead attempt to create a friendly and supportive classroom atmosphere that will encourage students to participate. TAs may have students discuss questions or issues in small groups so that Calvin Coolidge–type students will be more likely to participate. In whole-class discussions early in the semester, TAs may ask such students questions that call for a yes, no, or other limited response. Later in the semester, after the student has acquired confidence, questions calling for an elaborated response may be asked.

Students who are party persons enjoy the social aspects of class. Party persons love to talk, function in classes as social–emotional leaders, and view classes as "meet markets." They are attention-seekers for whom social concerns are more important than intellectual matters. These students are called "collaborative" in the learning styles literature; they learn best by sharing ideas, working in the company of others, and enjoying social interaction.[9]

The Party Person

Party persons can perform ably in class if they are given what they seek: love and attention. TAs can let party persons distribute handouts, organize a schedule for student oral reports, or present a summary of a previous period. By giving party persons recognition, TAs can provide the necessary motivation for them to achieve intellectual goals in addition to social ones.

Some students simply lack what it takes to make it in college, due to a lack of preparation. The unprepared student may lack necessary study skills, career direction, interest in the subject matter, or, possibly, native intelligence. Some may even be in college at their parents' insistence, rather than their own desire.

The Unprepared Student

The TA's responsibility is to get unprepared students to counseling services, to remedial services, and to other testing and tutoring services on campus. In many universities, information about such services is included in a TA handbook. When such information is not freely available, TAs may request it from the dean of students' office.

The Preoccupied Student

Students may be preoccupied with nonacademic pursuits: Greek activities, intercollegiate athletics, work, dating, family, drinking, or pumping iron. Second-semester seniors are notorious for "senior slump"—the feeling that they have had enough of school and that it is time to party before entering the "real world." Preoccupied students may come to TAs with a veritable plethora of excuses for late papers, nonattendance, or shoddy work.

The TA's strategy in dealing with preoccupied students is to let them know that they are not going to get away with it—that their grades will suffer if they do not start attending class regularly and doing the assignments. Once the TA has established the policy, it must be enforced.

The Terrorist

A terrorist treats college professors and TAs with hostility, cynicism, and detachment. Terrorists are habitual rebels who sit in the back of the class, make cutting remarks, and generally disrupt class proceedings. Terrorists are frequently juniors or seniors who are taking required freshman-level classes and who feel that the class is beneath their dignity. The student learning style literature terms these students "avoidants." Such students are "uninterested . . . by what goes on in classes," are "generally turned off by classroom activities," and "do not like enthusiastic teachers."[10]

Terrorists should not be taken lightly, especially if they are bright and verbally facile. A college professor once said to a terrorist, "If you don't wish to listen, maybe you'd like to teach the class." The terrorist replied, "What's the topic?" When the professor stated "meandering streams," the terrorist noted, "I can hack that," came to the front of the classroom, and delivered a thirty-minute lecture, accented by the professor's mannerisms, on meandering streams. He also excused the class fifteen minutes early to go observe a small stream on the north campus. The embarrassed professor tagged along.

TAs who are victims of terrorists cannot ignore the situation since terrorists can destroy the learning environment for all students. The most civilized way to deal with a terrorist is to arrange a private conference. During the conference, the TA should openly express how the terrorist's actions make him or her feel. Approaching a terrorist on a person-to-person level sometimes causes him or her to behave in a decent manner.

This strategy is not, however, universally effective. When a terrorist persists in expressing contempt for a course and/or a TA, he or she should be told to drop the course. As a last resort, the TA may ask the course director to speak with the terrorist in a firm manner.

Aggressive, verbally facile TAs who are victims of terrorists may be tempted to respond in kind by berating the terrorist with ridicule, name calling, and insults. While such hostile weapons may silence the terrorist, their use does little for the TA's image as a mature and responsible person.

Besides understanding and relating to different student personality types, TAs must follow certain principles when interacting with students. This section offers four guidelines for fostering positive TA–student relations.

Guidelines for Healthy TA–Student Relations

Get to Know Your Students

At large state universities, TAs are frequently the only instructors freshmen and sophomores get to know. By being approachable, TAs can help reduce the impersonality of a large institution. They may offer students course and career advice, emotional support, and letters of recommendation.

There are also sound academic reasons for getting to know students. Students who know that the TA has learned their names will feel a part of the class. Their enthusiasm for the class will be greater, as will their willingness to participate. Also, TAs who do not know their students' names will be unable to call on students in class.

There are various ways to learn student names. The first class meeting could be partially devoted to learning student names (rather than excusing students early). One method for learning names is to have students provide relevant personal information on file cards. After collecting the cards the TA may call each student's name and share some of the other information on the card as he or she attempts to associate the name with the person. The TA might even engage in a colloquy with each student. The point is to learn memorable information about each student and to create a positive atmosphere in the classroom. TAs can use the cards throughout the semester to match names, faces, and backgrounds.

Another approach is to have pairs of students interview each other. After a few minutes the students can introduce their partners to the rest of the class, revealing such information as major, hometown, year in college, and reason for taking the class. This method is likely to result in greater information being disclosed to the class than if students introduce themselves. Also, the focus is on student–student interaction, rather than on TA–student colloquy.

Another opening-day technique is to play "the name game." The first student introduces himself or herself and uses a mnemonic device to make his or her name memorable. The next person then repeats the name of the person in front of him or her and then introduces himself or herself with an appropriate mnemonic device. Once the last student in the class has named all of the other students and introduced himself or herself, the next step is to point to students out of order to see if students introduced at the beginning of the game can identify students who were introduced late in the game. Through the name game, students learn the names of fellow students, not simply the TA's name; such familiarity contributes to a positive classroom environment.

Requiring office hour visits, talking to students before and after class, and saying hello to students on the street, at the library, or at the gym are other ways a TA may learn student names. Receiving and returning exams is also an opportunity to move from 90 percent success to 100 percent success in name recognition (and to do so in a nonembarrassing manner to the TA or the student).

Don't Get to Know Them Biblically

Sexual harassment is a serious problem in universities, and it is receiving increased attention. One recent survey indicated that "one in six female graduate students in psychology had sexual contact with a professor while working on a graduate degree."[11] Sexual harassment is not, however, limited to male professors harassing female graduate students; TAs of both sexes may harass or be harassed by undergraduate students and professors of the opposite or the same sex.

Various definitions of sexual harassment have been offered, including "unwanted sexual comments, unwanted sexual overtones, offensive sexual materials, unwelcome fondling, and sexual assault."[12] Another definition is that sexual harassment is "promotion of stereotypes, unnecessary touching, patting, pinching, leering and/or ogling, sexual demands accompanied by implied or overt threats."[13]

Obviously, TAs should be very circumspect in their dealings with students. Charges of sexual harassment may be taken to court; even if not proven, an accusation would be very damaging to a TA. Many universities sponsor workshops for instructors on avoiding actions that may be interpreted as sexual harrassment.

In addition to avoiding such actions, TAs must also be very careful when dealing with students who are attracted to them. Although most universities do not have a formal rule prohibiting TAs from dating students, such behavior is clearly not a good idea. Students are often young and impressionable and can be hurt by an aborted romance with a TA. Also, TAs who date students will find themselves facing a conflict of interest when assigning grades. The MIT response to TAs who wonder if they should ask students "out for coffee or dinner and a show" and "see where it leads" is official and brief—"Don't."[14]

Inevitably, TAs communicate how they feel about students by how they act toward them. To be effective, TAs should display genuine respect and friendliness toward students. In order to have positive relations with students, TAs must think highly of them. TAs should avoid sarcasm and put-downs. Most students will respond (either positively or negatively) to a TA's self-fulfilling prophecy about their abilities and levels of maturity. TAs must believe in their students' abilities to learn the course material and participate effectively in class.

Communicate Genuine Respect

Communicating respect for students also involves respecting privacy. Grades should be kept anonymous. Posted exam scores and final grades should list only student numbers, not names. Exams should be returned only to the student; they should not be given to a student's friend or left in a pile outside the TA's office. TAs also should not make comments about a student to another student.

For those students who face the normal problems of adjustment to college, the TA's role is to be understanding. For students with more serious emotional and/or academic problems, the role of the TA is to refer students to the proper agencies. Some students may be contemplating suicide or abortion, may not know English as a native language, may have dyslexia, or may lack effective study skills. While TAs may be called upon to lend a sympathetic ear, they cannot be expected to be counselors for all of these problems. Instead, their responsibility is to refer students to the emotional and academic counseling services available on campus.

Communicate Genuine Concern

The communication of genuine concern by TAs frequently takes place during office hours. The TA's office provides an opportunity for the university's "shield of impersonality to be broken."[15] It is a forum for discussing both personal and academic problems.

Many TAs find that few students come to office hours.[16] This may be an indication that few students have concerns, problems, or questions, or it may indicate that they do not feel comfortable approaching the instructor. The more likely possibility is the latter. Students may be encouraged to come to office hours by direct written or oral invitation. Students will also be more likely to visit if they perceive the TA to be friendly, competent, and approachable and if the TA's office hours are convenient (at least three hours a week, at different times and days).

When students come to visit, TAs should create an atmosphere in which relaxed communication can occur. Students should be warmly welcomed and should receive the TA's full attention. Small talk can help break the ice and establish rapport.

Relating to Professors

In addition to relating to students, TAs must establish effective interpersonal relationships with members of the faculty. Relating to course directors and supervisors presents a new set of challenges for the TA.

Importance of the TA–Professor Relationship

Getting along with the supervising professor is extremely important. First, it will affect the overall success of the course. If the TA and the professor are not communicating, it will be difficult for them to blend the various components of instruction. Also, students can sense any rift between a professor and a TA and will attempt to exploit it. TAs who cannot communicate with the professor will be unable to relay the feelings of the students toward the class. TAs who are not part of the course decision-making process because of a lack of faculty–TA communication will not be of optimum help to students.

Second, a poor faculty–TA relationship could affect the TA's graduate student career. The supervising professor may write an unfavorable letter of evaluation (perhaps leading to nonreappointment as a TA). Negative appraisal of the graduate student as a TA may affect a professor's judgment of the graduate student's performance as a classroom student, as a writer of comprehensive examinations, and as a dissertation writer. Earning a reputation as a poor or noncooperative TA could have extremely damaging consequences for a TA's graduate career.

Open communication between the professor and the teaching assistant can be mutually rewarding.

Third, a faculty–TA relationship could affect the TA's career in a positive way. The TA who performs duties well and gets along with the supervising professor will probably gain a lifelong colleague, from whom letters of recommendation, professional guidance, and emotional support may be obtained.

Clearly, getting along with the professor is important. It can, however, be difficult since the TA is caught in the middle. To the student, the TA is a professor; to the professor, the TA is a student. The TA operates as a confidant to and buffer between professors and students, listening to the complaints of each about the other but being careful not to reveal what should not be revealed. Also, TAs and professors may disagree about standards. TAs who are generous graders, for example, may gain favor with students at the expense of losing stature with the professor.

One possible source of difficulty between professor and TA is the style of the professor, which may not be appropriate to the needs and desires of the TA. Some professors are reluctant to share decision-making powers, others believe that all members of a course instructional staff should participate in the decision-making process, and still others are willing to turn over major decision-making responsibilities to TAs.

Course Director Style as a Source of Potential Difficulty

The Authoritarian   Authoritarian course directors have strong convictions about the manner in which their courses should be taught. If in charge of a multisection course, the authoritarian is likely to prepare a common syllabus, provide handouts for all sections, prepare common examinations to be used in all sections, hold frequent staff meetings, and observe each TA one or more times during the semester. Similarly, the authoritarian professor using TAs in discussion or laboratory sections will require TAs to attend all lectures, will provide all materials that TAs will require in discussion or laboratory sections, will write all course examinations, and will devise a common scale for assigning grades for examinations. While the authoritarian professor may seem dictatorial, circumstances may warrant this style. Professors who use beginning TAs, or TAs who are teaching out of their areas of primary expertise, are well advised to provide considerable direction. Such TAs usually appreciate the direction and dedication of an authoritarian course director. The authoritarian style is not as well received by experienced TAs or by TAs who are firmly grounded in the subject matter field they are teaching. At some point, TAs need room to try out their own planning skills and their own creative approaches to teaching.

The Democrat   Democratic course directors believe that all members of an instructional staff should have input into all aspects of the decision-making process. When directing a multisection course, the democrat will distribute a sample syllabus to TAs but will encourage them to revise it to make it consistent with their approaches. Democrats invite TAs to serve on textbook selection committees, to contribute test items for all course examinations, and to work together with the professor to shape all examinations. When using TAs in laboratory sections, the democratic professor invites TAs to help prepare the schedule of laboratory experiments. Lab TAs meet periodically with the professor to talk about progress and to share ideas for making the laboratory experience more enjoyable and productive for students. Similarly, when using TAs in discussion sections, the democratic professor and his or her TAs meet frequently to discuss problems and progress and to talk about questions and response strategies for upcoming section meetings. While TAs have greater freedom working with a democratic course director than with an authoritarian course director, they are likely to have to work harder and to attend more and longer meetings. TAs who subscribe to the "just tell me what to do and I'll do it" philosophy will feel frustration in a course directed by a democratic professor.

The Libertarian   Libertarian professors believe in the doctrine of maximum freedom for their TAs. When directing a multisection course, libertarians meet with their TAs at the beginning of each semester to say hello and answer any questions; other staff meetings occur only if TAs request them. Libertarians seldom, if ever, visit the laboratory or discussion sections of their TAs. Libertarian professors give the lectures; TAs are responsible for everything else. Experienced TAs, who are confident about their mastery of the subjects being taught, often feel very comfortable working with a libertarian course director. Libertarians presume that their TAs are competent teachers who can function with a good deal of independence. TAs who are neither competent nor confident are likely to feel that they are being sent into battle by libertarian course directors, with neither adequate training nor sufficient logistical support.[17]

TA Behavior as a Source of Potential Difficulty

The TA–faculty relationship is also difficult because there are so many ways for a TA to go wrong. TAs may alienate professors by giving negative impressions such as those that follow.

Being Irresponsible   TAs can exhibit irresponsibility in several ways. There is no easier way for TAs to lose the respect of students and the course supervisor (and earn a reputation as a flake) than to be chronically tardy or absent. Being inattentive during lectures by the course director is also irresponsible. So, too, is failing to grade exams on time or employing erratic or idiosyncratic grading practices rather than following the professor's instructions.

Being Disinterested or Weak   TAs may succeed in alienating the professor by not seeming to care about the class—by failing to express enthusiasm, by not making the class a priority, or by not contributing to the planning of the class or the preparation of exams. TAs can also alienate professors by considering themselves too important to help out with "menial" tasks, such as distributing handouts or alphabetizing exams. Such TAs also consider faculty–TA staff meetings a waste of their time even though such meetings are factored into their work load. Finally, TA disinterest may express itself in weakness—in an inability to handle student problems. Professors resent having to handle minor administrative details or outlandish student requests that should be adjudicated by the TA.

Being Overly Aggressive   Just as TAs may be overly weak, they may be overly aggressive. TAs need to express their own ideas and suggestions enthusiastically without seeming to be disrespectful to the professor. TAs should not engage in unnecessary ideological, methodological, or pedagogical disputes with the professor. TAs should not make cutting remarks about the professor during office hours, in discussion sections, or while giving a guest lecture. TAs should not make fun of the class textbook (especially if it was written by the professor!). TAs should avoid calling the professor frequently at home, especially at dinner time or late in the evening. Finally, TAs must learn to be diplomatic in reporting critical student remarks about the course. TAs must first distinguish between those comments that need to be reported and those that do not and must then make sure to communicate the criticism in a constructive and gracious manner.

The most important guideline for a healthy TA–professor relationship is to maintain open communication with the course director. TAs should keep professors aware of what is going on in discussion and laboratory sections. Student problems with course material and attitudes toward the class should be communicated. Also, TAs should ask specific questions of supervising faculty regarding expectations, grading responsibility, and TA autonomy.

Guidelines for Healthy TA-Professor Relations

Another way to avoid problems in the faculty–TA relationship is for TAs to be responsible. This means showing up for class on time, doing the assigned readings, and providing emotional, intellectual, and logistical support for the professor. Niels Nielsen, recipient of an

In the course of their duties, TAs confer with members of the departmental support staff.

Outstanding Teaching Assistant Award from the University of California–Davis, advises TAs "to assume as active a role as possible . . . by looking for things that need to be done, rather than by waiting to be told to do something."[18]

Relating to Staff Members

TAs must also establish effective relationships with secretaries and other members of the support staff. Many TAs have never worked in a department before and thus do not understand the rules of departmental politics. The key fact is that secretaries and other members of the support staff are very important people. Secretaries type exams and handouts, take messages, report physical plant problems to the proper authorities, arrange for classroom assignments, process add–drop information, order textbooks, and perform a myriad of other functions. Secretaries are also a great source of information about departmental policies and procedures. Similarly, departmental custodians, engineers, librarians, and other support staff perform important services and should be treated with respect. TAs should not make unreasonable demands on support personnel. TAs should not ask that projects be completed on the spot; rather, substantial lead time should be allowed. TAs who ask support personnel to undertake major tasks should acknowledge that fact and express gratitude. TAs should observe protocol when asking for work to be done: projects should be given to the person in charge for disbursement, and (when appropriate) the professor's name should be used when making requests.

Summary

TAs must establish effective interpersonal relationships with a number of people. They must relate to students of such varying personalities as the self-motivated learner, the respectful learner, the submissive student, the paranoid student, the Calvin Coolidge type, the party person, the unprepared student, the preoccupied student, and the terrorist. When relating to students, TAs should get to know them by name, be careful to avoid sexual harassment, communicate genuine respect, and communicate genuine concern. When relating to professors, TAs should recognize the importance of such relationships; be aware of the potential difficulty of relating to authoritarian, democratic, and libertarian course directors; avoid being irresponsible, disinterested, or overly aggressive in their own behaviors; and seek to maintain open communication. Finally, TAs should treat all members of the support staff in a courteous and considerate manner.

Notes

1. *Manual for Teaching Assistants,* College of Letters and Science, University of Wisconsin–Madison, September 1985, pp. 3, 1, and 2.
2. This typology was influenced by Richard Mann, et al., who present an eight-part grouping of student types: independent students, heroes, compliant students, snipers, discouraged workers, silent students, attention-seeking students, and anxious-dependents. *The College Classroom: Conflict, Change, and Learning* (New York: John Wiley & Sons, 1970), pp. 147–223.
3. Barbara Schneider Fuhrmann and Anthony F. Grasha, *A Practical Handbook for College Teachers* (Boston: Little, Brown and Company, 1983), pp. 114–15.
4. Glenn Johnson, *Analyzing College Teaching* (Nanchaca, Tex.: Sterling Swift Publishing Company, 1976).
5. Fuhrmann and Grasha, p. 123.
6. Fuhrmann and Grasha, p. 123.
7. Barbara Schneider Fuhrman and Anthony F. Grasha, *A Practical Handbook for College Teachers* (Boston: Little, Brown and Company, 1983), p. 123. Used with permission.
8. Fuhrmann and Grasha, p. 122.
9. Fuhrmann and Grasha, p. 122.
10. Fuhrmann and Grasha, p. 122.
11. Scott Heller, "One in Six Female Graduate Students in Psychology Reports Having Sexual Contact with a Professor," *Chronicle of Higher Education,* February 16, 1986, p. 23.
12. Flyer, University of Wisconsin–Madison, "TA Workshop on Sexual Harassment," April 5, 1986.
13. Flyer, Ada James Women's Center, University of Wisconsin–Madison, "Stop Sexual Harassment Now!" no date.

14. *The TA at UCLA: 1984–1985 Handbook* (Los Angeles: University of California, Los Angeles, 1984), p. 29.

15. The advice offered in this paragraph and the one following was influenced by *The TA at UCLA,* p. 29.

16. The three types of professorial style are not, of course, mutually exclusive. Some professors may represent a blend of two of these styles. In addition, some professors change their styles according to the context in which they find themselves. This system for classifying professorial styles is based on the autocratic, democratic, and laissez-faire distinction often used in small-group literature. For a discussion of these styles see Marvin E. Shaw, *Group Dynamics: The Psychology of Small Group Behavior,* 3d ed. (New York: McGraw-Hill, 1981), pp. 326–31.

17. *TA Handbook* (Davis: Teaching Resources Center, University of California, Davis, no date), p. 5.

4

Planning for Instruction

"Before your first class session try to meet with your supervising professor. The professor should brief you on the course's content. It is best if such an orientation meeting is planned well in advance of the first class and if it involves all the course's TAs, so that everyone is clear on . . . [his or her] responsibilities and can prepare properly for the semester. If your professor has not set up such a meeting, you should feel free to request one. If the professor is unable to conduct this orientation session, TAs can still help each other prepare for the course by holding their own meeting in which veteran TAs explain to their less experienced colleagues what to expect in teaching the course."[1]

Learning to Teach: A Handbook
for Teaching Assistants
at U.C. Berkeley

Effective teaching begins with careful TA planning.

This quotation from the University of California, Berkeley handbook stresses the importance of TA planning and suggests that such planning should begin well in advance of the first class meeting. It should also be noted that planning is not a one-time phenomenon. Planning continues throughout the term; it is a weekly if not daily reality of TA life.

Without meaning to do so, the author of this quotation also indicates another reality of TA planning: TAs normally plan in the shadows of course directors. In some cases professors provide a good deal of direction for their TAs. In other cases TAs are expected to plan with a good deal of autonomy.

Whatever the contingencies of a particular assignment, in the long run TAs will wish to acquire skills related to a number of dimensions of instructional planning: determining a starting point, identifying instructional objectives, choosing instructional strategies, devising instructional materials, and creating instructional plans.

Determining a Starting Point

When TAs are asked what it means to teach, their responses suggest three primary approaches to teaching: "teaching as content, teaching as process, and teaching as motivation."[2] This finding is consistent with an earlier belief that all teaching falls somewhere along a continuum ranging from subject-centered to student-centered.

Most college teachers have a strong subject-matter orientation. As they plan for instruction, they partition course information into manageable chunks, which become the topics of lectures. In this approach, lectures are the building blocks out of which a course is constructed.

Beginning with Content

TAs who have a content orientation believe that "course subject matter and mastery of that material by students"[3] is what teaching is all about. In planning for teaching, such TAs look first at the body of content to be taught. They ask themselves questions about the subject matter, such as: What are the major components of this body of knowledge? Should these components be presented in a certain order? What concepts must a student acquire if the content is to be mastered?

TAs who are assigned to large lecture courses without discussion or laboratory sections usually find that the professors of such courses are operating out of a content orientation. In order to assist the professor competently, the TA will also need to adopt this orientation. When preparing handouts, devising test items, or grading student work, the TA must have a clear conception of the content being taught.

Beginning with Process

TAs with a process orientation, while recognizing the importance of content, are not interested in simply teaching information for its own sake. Rather, "these TAs . . . want their students to leave class not merely having memorized or understood facts, concepts, and procedures pertinent to the course, but better able to think and to process information."[4] They are more interested in student use of knowledge than they are in student possession of knowledge.

Many TA appointments call for a process orientation. Laboratory section TAs are concerned primarily with their students' abilities to use information in solving problems or performing experiments. TAs in composition, foreign language, and speech communication courses are interested in improving the communication skills of their students. TAs in discussion sections across the curriculum are expected to challenge students to apply knowledge rather than simply recall it.

When taking this approach, TAs begin by asking themselves questions about the process in which they wish their students to engage. What should my students be able to do with their acquired knowledge at the conclusion of this course? What components of the process may be identified? In what sequence should these components be taught? What role does practice play in the development of student thinking or performance skills?

Beginning with Students   TAs who subscribe to a student-centered approach believe that student motivation is at the heart of learning.[5] Since affect accompanies and influences all learning, these TAs believe that affect should receive serious consideration in the decision-making process. Thus, they begin planning by asking questions such as: Why are my students taking this course? What would they like to learn from this course? What materials will they find most interesting? What learning activities will they enjoy participating in?

The most obvious use of this approach is in directed study courses. In such courses, students contract with professors who agree to supervise a program of study for them. Students identify what they wish to learn or accomplish; professors help them to pursue their goals.

TAs become involved in courses calling for student-centered approaches in a number of ways. First, senior TAs are often used to coordinate undergraduate internships in off-campus settings. Students who are placed in field experiences in business, school, or government settings return to campus one evening each week for a lecture on a relevant topic by the TA and to share experiences and feelings. TAs may also follow the interns into the work setting to evaluate their performances.

In some departments TAs are assigned to courses that naturally attract students who are motivated to acquire the knowledge or skill in question. TAs in the fine arts, for example, work with students who wish to learn to act, dance, write creatively, paint, sing, sculpt, or engage in glass blowing. In many of these courses, students are permitted to choose the particular projects or events they will pursue. Even in more traditional laboratory sections and discussion sections, TAs who are student-centered find ways to adapt instruction to the needs and interests of their students.

Identifying Instructional Objectives

Whatever a TA's starting point, he or she will need to identify instructional objectives. It is a central part of the planning process. One handbook suggests that TAs should start by writing instructional objectives and should then develop a course outline.[6] This order is probably appropriate for the student-centered approach since the TA and the student normally talk about the objectives of the program of directed study or the field experience during an initial conference.

TAs are just as likely, however, to begin with a syllabus, a textbook, and/or a laboratory manual or discussion guide. This is what course directors often provide. Beginning with this kind of material, the TA must decide what instructional objectives may be achieved in the course.

The secret to becoming an excellent planner is to master the art of identifying and clarifying instructional objectives. The secret to mastering instructional objectives is practice. If instructional objectives are clearly written, and if objectives are provided for everything the instructor considers important, students will no longer have to play guessing games. Instructional objectives are also of value to college teachers when communicating about course goals with each other. And, finally, clearly expressed objectives help instructors to choose instructional and assessment strategies.

The Nature and Importance of Instructional Objectives

Writing clear instructional objectives is not a difficult task. Once TAs understand the form, most can create a set of objectives with relative ease.

The Form of Instructional Objectives

A key phrase that occurs in instructional objectives is "the student will be able to." To this key phrase, TAs need only add bits of language designed to clarify their expectations. Three kinds of additional information are normally provided: descriptions of desired behaviors, statements about conditions, and statements about standards.[7] Each of these three kinds of additional information will be considered briefly.

Descriptions of Desired Behaviors   Descriptions of desired behaviors simply indicate what the student will be able to do after instruction. A description involves an action verb plus the object of the action. Consider the following examples of behaviors in the company of the key phrase:

> The student will be able to *differentiate between* nuclear fission and nuclear fusion.
> The student will be able to *list* the common types of figures of speech (e.g., metaphor, simile, etc.).
> The student will be able to *write* an informative essay.
> The student will be able to *identify* cloud formations by type.

In each of these examples, the instructional goal is relatively clear. This clarity is attributable to the use of verbs that identify observable behaviors.

Some college instructors are accustomed to using weak-kneed verbs to describe their goals. They use expressions such as know, understand, appreciate, grasp the significance of, really understand, and fully appreciate.[8] The problem with such expressions is that they point to internal states rather than to observable behavior. It is, after all, difficult to tell by observing students whether they have "developed a profound understanding of totalitarian systems."

Words that carry more precise meaning include write, recite, identify, differentiate, solve, construct, list, compare, and contrast.[9] Such words help to express objectives more clearly since they point to actions that students may demonstrate. For example, a political science TA might hope that his or her students will be able "to compare and contrast authoritarian and autocratic regimes."

The practice of specifying observable behavior in instructional objectives is not without controversy. Those who applaud such phrasing believe that it has caused curriculum designers "to pay more attention to measures of student achievement"[10] and caused instructors to clarify their own thinking about course goals. Critics, on the other hand, allege that such a practice has "distracted attention from the crucial question of what objectives are worthwhile to the subordinate one of how objectives should be written."[11] They have also charged that this practice shows a greater interest in what is countable than what counts.[12]

Pratt has offered a useful framework for understanding the controversy.[13] He distinguishes between instructional intent (objectives) and behavioral indicators (performance criteria). For example, the student's ability to "differentiate between nuclear fission and fusion" is a performance criterion for the objective of "creating student understanding of nuclear energy." Given this perspective, one may conclude that it is important to reflect upon both the value of a learning goal and the manner in which it may be measured. In the remainder of this chapter, the term instructional objective is used to refer to statements that specify performance criteria.

Statements about Conditions   Statements about conditions identify the circumstances surrounding student performance of the desired behavior. Conditions are often specified at the beginning of objectives, as in the following examples:

> *Given a laboratory setting and a chemistry lab manual,* the student will be able to determine the identity of an unknown substance.
>
> *Without the use of notes or other materials,* the student will be able to differentiate between operant and classical conditioning.
>
> *By the end of the course,* the student will be able to identify and indicate the significance of changes in the American political system during the Civil War era.

Conditions may also be placed at other points in the objective, as in the following example:

> *Given sixty minutes,* the student will be able to write an essay *in French* identifying similarities and differences among Hugo, Beaudelaire, and Balzac in terms of style, themes, and genre.

Wherever conditions are placed in objectives, they help to clarify the TA's expectations and instructional intent.

Statements about Standards   Standards are the final component of instructional objectives. Standards specify the criteria to be used in judging student behavior. In some cases the standard may involve *time*. For example, an instructional objective for a physical conditioning course might have the following objective:

> By the end of the term, the student will be able to run a mile *in less than seven minutes*.

In other cases the standard may involve the number of student responses desired. For example, an instructional objective for a women's studies course might have the following objective:

> Students will be able to chronicle, in written form, *ten* major events in the struggle against sexism.

In still other cases the standard may specify the *percentage* of correct responses desired. For example, an instructional objective for a Spanish course might have the following objective:

> Given a list of idioms, the student will be able to translate *80 percent* of them accurately.

Since standards may take many forms, the examples provided in this section are meant to be representative rather than exhaustive.

The Cognitive Level of Instructional Objectives

Since instruction occurs at varying cognitive levels, TAs will need to write objectives for the several levels. The best-known system for classifying behaviors in the cognitive domain was invented by Benjamin Bloom and his colleagues over thirty years ago.[14] In essence, the system consists of a hierarchy of six levels of cognitive behavior, each level subsuming all lesser levels.

The lowest rung on the cognitive ladder involves *recall*[15] of some form of knowledge: facts, means of dealing with facts, precepts, concepts. The second rung involves *comprehension*. At this level the student must translate, paraphrase, explain, or summarize knowledge to demonstrate that it is understood. The third rung involves the *application* of knowledge to new and/or particular situations. The fourth rung, *analysis*, involves dissecting a whole in order to reveal its constituent elements. The fifth rung, *synthesis*, involves creating some unique plan, message, theme, or construction. The top rung on the cognitive ladder is *evaluation*. At this level students are expected to make critical judgments about things based on internal and external evidence.

To test your understanding of this information, identify the cognitive level represented by each of the following objectives:

> Without the use of notes, the student will be able to define, in twenty-five words or less, the term photosynthesis such that the student's definition is similar to but not an exact replica of the textbook definition.
>
> Given samples of five rocks and the names of five rocks, the student will be able to match the rock samples with their names with 100 percent accuracy.
>
> Without the use of notes or other materials, the student will be able to identify the titles of ten works attributed to Shakespeare.

The first objective is at the comprehension level since the student is being asked to paraphrase a definition of photosynthesis. The second objective is at the application level since the student is being asked to apply his or her knowledge of rocks and their attributes to an actual collection of rocks. Finally, the third objective is at the recall level since it merely asks the student to name ten works of Shakespeare considered in the course.

Now that you have had experience analyzing objectives, you may wish to try your hand at synthesizing some objectives of your own. You can do so by selecting some classification system from your major field of study (e.g., types of governments, movie genres, types of evergreen trees) and completing the following objectives. Insert the number of objects in the system plus the title of the system (e.g., *six movie genres*) into the blank spaces provided in each objective. You will find it necessary to make modest adjustments.

> **Recall:** Without the use of notes, the student will be able to identify the _____ _____ .
>   (number) (title of classification system)
>
> **Comprehension:** When called upon to do so, the student will be able to define in his or her own words the _____ _____
>   (number) (title of classifi-
> _____ , such that the definitions parallel those given in the
> cation system)
> text.

Application: Given examples of the _____ _____
(number) (title of classification
_____ , the student will be able to identify each example by type
system)
with 80-percent accuracy.

Analysis: Given a _____
(place where objects in the classification system
_____ , the student will determine which of the
are normally found)
_____ _____ are present.
(number) (title of classification system)

Most TAs find that with a little practice they are able to write objectives
for varying cognitive levels. If you feel confident about your skill, you
may select another classification system from your major field of study
and write your own objectives at the recall, comprehension, application,
and analysis levels. You can also try to write synthesis and evaluation
objectives for this same content.

In the next section you will learn how an awareness of the cognitive
level of instructional objectives can help you to choose instructional
strategies. In chapter 7 you will learn how this same knowledge can improve your ability to ask varied and provocative questions when leading
class discussions.

Choosing Instructional Strategies

Once instructors have determined and clarified their instructional objectives they are in an excellent position to choose their instructional
strategies. For example, instructors in survey courses will probably discover that their instructional objectives are almost exclusively at the recall
and comprehension levels. Given this situation, the course can probably
be taught as a lecture course with enrollment determined by student
demand, size of available hall, availability of TAs to help with course
administration, and the lecturing talents of the instructor. If the instructor is skillful in organizing and presenting lectures, recall- and
comprehension-level objectives may be achieved without the necessity of
discussion sections.

In other courses, however, instructors are not content if their students merely recall and comprehend knowledge; they want them to use
knowledge by applying it to new situations or by analyzing relevant objects, events, concepts, or theories. In such cases the list of objectives for
a course is likely to include some at the application and analysis levels
as well as some at the recall and comprehension levels. When courses
with such objectives are taught in a large lecture format, discussion and/
or laboratory sections are usually necessary. The experiments provided

in most laboratory manuals function at the application level, with occasional forays into analysis. In discussion sections, however, TAs often misunderstand their function. They simply ask recall- and comprehension-level questions of their students rather than forcing students to use knowledge in application- and analysis-level activities. Perhaps this explains why students are often absent from discussion section meetings.

When the instructional objectives for a course include objectives at the synthesis and evaluation levels, small classes of an autonomous nature are often called for. Among the courses that fit this type are classes in foreign language, composition, public speaking, filmmaking, and literary criticism. Almost all upper-division courses reflect some instructional goals at these higher cognitive levels.

Devising Instructional Materials

In addition to helping instructors choose basic instructional strategies, objectives can also help them to devise instructional materials. The use of objectives in this way is strongly influenced by the TA's assignment.

Devising Materials Using a Content Approach

Imagine that you are a TA for a large lecture course. How can you use instructional objectives to improve the quality of instruction provided? First of all, you could identify the apparent objectives of the course (if the course director has not done so) and distribute them to students (with the course director's approval). Since the course objectives are likely to be at the recall and comprehension levels, you probably will not be able to devise highly creative and cognitively challenging supplementary learning activities. Still, there are several things you could do that would be of value to the students and that would not get in the course director's way. For example, each of the following actions would contribute to student recall and comprehension:

Outline a complex lecture given by the course director and distribute the outline at the next class meeting.

Provide a handout in which key terms in the course are defined.

Prepare a handout that compares, contrasts, or integrates lecture and textual materials.

While TAs who are employed to assist in large lecture courses are somewhat restricted in what they may contribute, intelligent and dedicated TAs find ways to improve the courses to which they are assigned.

Devising Materials Using a Process Approach

TAs who subscribe to the process approach find that a series of instructional objectives may help them to devise learning materials. For example, imagine that you are a TA in an autonomous section of a composition or public speaking course. Imagine further that you decide your students should learn about some common methods for organizing ideas. As a systematic type, you would sit down at your desk and create a set of instructional objectives reflecting diverse cognitive levels. Your objectives might look like this:

Recall

1. Without the use of notes, the student will be able to identify at least six of the eight common patterns of organization (chronological, spatial, topical, refutative, problem–solution, alternative, causal, and comparison/contrast).

Comprehension

2. When called upon to do so by the instructor, the student will be able to define a pattern of organization in his or her own words and with sufficient clarity that peers are able to name the pattern being defined.

Application

3. Given a list of topics, purposes, and audiences, the student will be able to indicate the patterns that seem most appropriate to those variables such that the student's choices match a key prepared in advance by the TA.

Analysis

4. Given a speech from *Vital Speeches,* the student will be able to identify the pattern of organization used to organize the main points. The student's response should either match the TA's response or should be shown to be a plausible alternative response in subsequent discussion.

Synthesis

5. At the conclusion of this unit, the student will be able to construct an outline of the body of a speech such that the patterns used to develop the main points and first-level subpoints are clearly identifiable by the TA.

Evaluation

6. Given texts of two expository essays, the student will be able to compare the relative effectiveness of the organizational patterns employed. The student will provide comparative judgments about the appropriateness, efficiency, and artistry of the two texts.[16]

Having specified your objectives with precision, you are now in an excellent position to determine the instructional materials that you must devise.

In order for students to accomplish objective 1, you might just lecture about patterns of organization, expecting students to name the patterns when called upon to do so. To ensure that they are learning to do what is specified in objective 2, you could have them practice defining the patterns of organization. To prepare students for objective 3, you could specify a topic, a purpose, and an audience for a speech and ask them to identify appropriate patterns of organization. To prepare students for objective 4, you could give them copies of speeches to analyze in small groups. To prepare students for objective 5, you could let them work in pairs, constructing outlines of different topics to gain practice in using various patterns. Finally, to prepare students for objective 6, you could hand out copies of expository essays and make comparative judgments about them as a way of modeling appropriate evaluative behaviors.

It should be clear that instructional objectives provide clear guidance about the instructional materials one should devise. The six objectives cited provide the basis for approximately two periods of instruction. Similar objectives for all areas of skill relevant to oral or written composition would point the way to a fully developed course plan for a public speaking or written composition course.

Devising Materials Using a Student-centered Approach

In its pure form, the student-centered approach begins with a student who has a learning goal he or she wishes to accomplish. The student's task is to find a professor who can help her or him to define and complete the task and to award credits for directed study.

Since TAs are normally not allowed to contract with undergraduate students for such purposes, the student-centered approach in its pure form is not likely to be used by TAs. TAs do, however, teach courses in which students are expected to complete a program of independent study leading to a course term paper or acceptable alternative project. Imagine, for example, that you are an experienced graduate student in political science who has been assigned to be the lecturer for "Introduction to International Relations." The course requires each student to write a five- to eight-page paper. Early in the term, one of your students requests that she be permitted to complete an alternative course project. Since she will be program chair for the International Relations Club next term, she would like to plan a series of debates on crucial issues in international relations. Since her proposed project has obvious merit and will require as much or more work than the regular term project, you are happy to agree. Now, how do you proceed?

TAs are often called upon to help students plan and carry out individual projects.

Define the Task   In an early conference with the student, the task should be clearly defined. What is the ultimate goal of the learner? What specific objectives does the student wish to achieve? Will draft copy for an International Relations Club brochure be acceptable to you as the final paper? What kinds of content will be included in such a brochure? Will the two debaters for each issue be contacted before the end of the term?

Identify the Stages of the Task   At the same meeting, you would probably wish to encourage the student to identify everything that must be done if the task is to be successfully accomplished. As you interact with the student it becomes apparent that she will have to identify five crucial issues for the five-part series, phrase a proposition for each of the issues, decide on a debate format, secure speakers, and prepare draft copy of the brochure.

Plan a Work Schedule   Since a term has a way of passing rapidly, both for instructors and undergraduates, it is important that a work schedule be planned. In this case the student might decide to have the major issues identified by Friday of the fourth week, the propositions phrased and the format determined by Friday of the sixth week, and the speakers secured by Friday of the eighth week, leaving the rest of the term to prepare brochure copy.

Identify Sources of Needed Information   You will also wish to help the student identify sources of information. The issues, for example, could be determined by looking for topics that have been given most attention in professional journals in the past year, by interviewing professors in the political science department, or by surveying members of the International Relations Club. The format for phrasing propositions could be determined by looking at several books on argumentation and debate and/or by interviewing persons who have special expertise in this area.

Provide Feedback as the Project Unfolds   As the student's work unfolds, it is important to meet periodically to discuss progress and provide feedback. In this case you would probably meet on each of the deadline dates established in the work schedule. Other meetings could be scheduled as necessary.

Creating Instructional Plans

Anyone who has gathered instructional plans from across the curriculum of a large university has undoubtedly concluded that instructional plans have not been standardized. In a sense, one can take pleasure from the fact that administrators have not succeeded in standardizing something as personal and important as instructional plans. After all, the form of a plan should be largely determined by its function. Still, it is apparent that many who teach on American college campuses have given little attention to the functions their plans, or at least their syllabi, may serve. In this section, consideration will be given to three types of plans that are commonly created: the syllabus, the section plan, and class plans.

The Syllabus

The syllabus is the most popular plan format in American colleges and universities. Students expect to receive a course syllabus at the first meeting of each course they take; in fact, if instructors arrive at the first class meeting without a syllabus, they had better be ready to explain its absence. A syllabus can help students decide if they have chosen wisely. It also identifies such essential information as examination dates, paper due dates, reading assignments, and course format. Some syllabi also include such additional information as the instructor's name, office address, office hours, and office phone number. Many syllabi include descriptive information about the course such as general course objectives, a rationale for course organization, criteria for major assignments, grading procedures, and attendance expectations.

The Section Plan

TAs who teach autonomous lecture sections are expected either to distribute a common course syllabus or to adapt a sample syllabus to their particular needs. When a common syllabus is used, TAs may supplement the syllabus, either orally or in writing, with personal information.

TAs in charge of laboratory or discussion sections in large lecture courses may reveal their plans in a number of ways. In some instances, discussion and laboratory section topics are included in the general course syllabus. This is likely when the course director is an authoritarian. In other cases, TAs distribute discussion or laboratory schedules either at the first section meeting or periodically as new units are introduced. Such schedules normally include the date, the topic or experiment, and the assignment.

Class Plans

Unlike the syllabus and the section plan, which are intended for distribution to students and others, class plans are intended for the personal use of the professor or TA. Such plans reflect the instructor's considered judgment about what should occur during a given class period. Among the items that may be included in a class plan are a review of the last section or lecture, a preview of what will happen during the present period, ideas designed to stimulate student interest, a list of instructional objectives or goals, a lecture outline, reminders to use supplementary materials, a list of major instructional activities, a list of questions to be asked or experiments to be completed, and a list of such concluding activities as a summary or a preview of the next class meeting.

Summary

Planning for instruction involves making a series of decisions. The first level of decision making involves determining a starting point. Some TAs begin by looking at course content, others assume a process orientation, and still others begin by considering student needs and interests. At some point TAs will find it useful to write instructional objectives that clearly identify desired learning outcomes. Instructional objectives consist of the words "the student will be able to" plus descriptions of desired behavior, statements about conditions, and statements about standards. Instructional objectives may also be written at various cognitive levels: recall, comprehension, application, analysis, synthesis, and evaluation. Once instructors have determined and clarified their instructional goals, they are in an excellent position to choose their instructional strategies. Lower-order cognitive goals (recall and comprehension) can be achieved through lectures. When instructors also have objectives at the application and analysis levels, lecture courses are often supplemented by discussion and/or laboratory sections. When synthesis and evaluation objectives are present, smaller, autonomous classes are frequently called for. Instructional objectives also help TAs devise instructional materials. This is true whether using the content approach, the process approach, or the student-centered approach. Finally, TAs are expected to record their instructional choices in three kinds of instructional plans: syllabi, section plans, and class plans. TAs who use the information presented in this chapter can acquire excellent planning skills.

Notes

1. Robby Cohen, "Preparing for Your First Class," in *Learning to Teach: A Handbook for Teaching Assistants at U.C. Berkeley* (Berkeley: Graduate Assembly, University of California, 1985), p. 6.
2. Robert J. Menges and William C. Rando, "Graduate Teaching Assistants' Implicit Theories of Teaching," in *Institutional Responsibilities and Responses in the Employment and Education of Teaching Assistants: Readings from a National Conference,* general ed. Nancy Van Note Chism (Columbus: Center for Teaching Excellence, The Ohio State University, 1987), p. 84.
3. Menges and Rando, p. 84.
4. Menges and Rando, p. 84.
5. Menges and Rando, p. 86.
6. Michele Fisher, ed., *Teaching at Stanford: An Introductory Handbook* (Stanford, Calif.: Stanford University, 1983), p. 6.
7. We have taken the names of these components from Robert Kibler, Larry L. Barker, and David T. Miles, *Behavioral Objectives and Instruction* (Boston: Allyn and Bacon, 1970), p. 33. However, it should be noted that the source of instructional objectives to which all subsequent publications owe an intellectual debt is Robert F. Mager, *Preparing Instructional Objectives* (Palo Alto, Calif.: Fearon Publishers, 1962).
8. Mager, p. 11.
9. Mager, p. 11.
10. David Pratt, *Curriculum: Design and Development* (New York: Harcourt, Brace, Jovanovich, 1980), p. 182.
11. Pratt, pp. 182–83.
12. Pratt, p. 183, quotes economist Herman Daly's statement that it is important to "care about what counts, not about what is merely countable."
13. Pratt, pp. 181–83.
14. Benjamin S. Bloom, Mac D. Englehart, Edward J. Furst, Walker H. Hill, and David R. Krathwohl, *Taxonomy of Educational Objectives, Handbook I: Cognitive Domain* (New York: David McKay Company, 1956), pp. 201–7.
15. In the system devised by Bloom, et al., the lowest cognitive level is called knowledge rather than recall. We prefer the term recall since all cognitive levels involve knowledge.
16. The content of this set of objectives is based on the development provided by R. R. Allen and Ray E. McKerrow, *The Pragmatics of Public Communication,* 3d ed. (Dubuque, Iowa: Kendall/Hunt Publishing, 1985), pp. 64–74.

5

Creating a Supportive Classroom Environment

"We're usually all there when he walks in. He looks sort of embarrassed, stares down at the desk and asks if we have any questions. There's an awkward silence, like at a party where nobody can think of anything to say. Then he starts to work a problem from the homework. He talks to the blackboard in a steady even way. You can hear, but you can't tell what's important and what isn't. I can't follow one of the steps, but I'm afraid to say anything. Every now and then he says, O.K.?, but it doesn't mean anything and he doesn't stop. After a while you don't really understand much and wonder why you're there. I copy the stuff into my notebook—I'll probably be able to figure it out at home—but if it weren't for the exam I know I'd never look at it.

I guess I keep going because I know that otherwise I'd just waste the hour some other way. He knows his stuff all right, but it's like he's up front and we're back there and there's a glass wall between us."[1]

MIT undergradate student
The Torch or the Firehose?

However well TAs may plan for a class and however well they may "know their stuff," instruction is unlikely to be effective if TAs fail to establish a classroom environment that is conducive to student learning. The teaching assistant described in this quotation appears insensitive to the needs of his students. He simply walks into the classroom at the last minute, gives his students token attention, and proceeds with his presentation as if students were not present. He neither invites nor appears to desire interaction with his students. As a consequence, his students feel ignored and alienated.

To avoid such negative student reactions, TAs must be sensitive to the quality of the classroom environment; they must both recognize and accept responsibility for nonsupportive settings. Having done so, they may then create a supportive physical and psychological environment and encourage student involvement in classroom learning. Finally, TAs should recognize that the first day of instruction is especially important since it sets the stage for the remainder of the term.

Being Sensitive to the Quality of the Classroom Environment

Course supervisors, who travel from section to section to observe TAs at work, soon become aware of major differences in classroom environments. In some classrooms, the students and the TA arrive early and chat amiably about course- and noncourse-related matters. When the period begins, the TA and the students continue to relate to each other as people as they engage in animated discussion of course content. In other classrooms, students seem unaware of each other as people. While waiting for class to begin, they sit mute at their desks or quietly browse copies of the campus newspaper. As additional students arrive, no words of greeting or recognition are exchanged. The TA's arrival is, similarly, unmarked by verbal exchange. When the period begins, the TA seems formal and officious and the students seem distant and unresponsive. In some cases, TAs are totally unaware that their classroom environments are of less than ideal quality. In other cases, TAs recognize that all is not well but refuse to accept responsibility for the problem.

Recognizing a Nonsupportive Classroom Environment

A classroom environment is supportive when it is conducive to the achievement of instructional goals. Consequently, the attributes of a supportive environment differ across classrooms as instructional purposes or goals vary. For example, in a review section the TA is often expected to highlight and clarify the content of earlier lectures by the professor. Communication roles tend to be relatively fixed; the TA speaks and the students listen and take notes. A classroom environment is supportive of the review function if students have an unobstructed view of

The use of a multi-headed microscope creates an environment in which students can converse with the TA and each other while viewing common slides.

the TA and any visual materials he or she employs, if the TA is sufficiently interesting to sustain audience attention, and if the TA presents information in a clear and well-organized manner. A classroom environment is nonsupportive of the review function if a noisy heating system, messy visual materials, or wayward student conversations interfere with efficient transfer of information.

In discussion sections, however, it is desirable for communication roles to be variable rather than fixed. Students are expected to actively participate in the discussion—both initiating ideas and responding to the ideas of others. A classroom environment is conducive to discussion if it encourages student participation. A classroom environment is not conducive to a class discussion if the TA talks most of the time, if the furniture arrangement is inappropriate, or if the discussion is centered around trivial questions that do not inspire intellectual exchange.

In laboratory sections, it is expected that students will complete projects under the watchful eye of a TA facilitator. A laboratory environment is supportive if instructions are clearly given, if student work is carefully monitored by the TA, if students feel free to interact with the TA and each other as they complete learning tasks, and if students receive timely and thoughtful feedback concerning their work. A laboratory environment is not conducive if instructions are vague, if student interaction is discouraged, if the TA is aloof and unapproachable, or if student work is not evaluated in a fair and thorough manner.

Whatever the instructional purpose or setting, TAs will need to recognize the existence of forces that intrude on the learning process. It is impossible to solve a problem if one is not aware that a problem exists.

Accepting Responsibility for Environmental Quality

Even TAs who recognize the existence of a problem may fail to accept responsibility for doing anything about it. Fuhrmann and Grasha have noted the human tendency to "blame external things for our problems." They note:

> An instructor encountering a lack of interest or involvement in students typically blames the students, the classroom facilities, the time of day, the required nature of the course, or any other handy factor. What is usually ignored or overlooked is his or her personal responsibility for the lack of involvement.[2]

TAs have been known to complain, "I knock myself out writing exciting questions for discussion and they just sit there like lumps" or "This is exciting and important stuff, but all the students care about is whether it will be on the test. I can't believe these people!"

Rather than simply blaming the students or the circumstances, Fuhrmann and Grasha allege that "both personal factors and aspects of the situation are responsible for any behavior. To ignore one in favor of the other is to make a judgment error."[3] Thus, when TAs recognize the existence of a problem they should question their own responsibilities in the matter: In what ways may I be inhibiting interaction? Is it possible that my lectures are boring? What can I do to motivate greater student interest and involvement? By accepting responsibility, TAs can change unfavorable aspects of the situation.

Attending to the Physical Environment

Fred Steele notes that people who have "environmental competence" both recognize the importance of the physical environment to effective communication and alter physical settings to improve communication.[4] Unfortunately, Steele also notes that most people have a bias in favor of leaving things as they are.[5] Many TAs, for example, are willing to accept a classroom on its own terms; however the furniture is arranged and no matter what is written on the chalkboard, some TAs just proceed with the class meeting. Common sense suggests otherwise. A clear chalkboard is less visually distracting than one containing the notes from a previous period. But better yet, the TA might use the chalkboard to preview the period, to note an upcoming assignment, or to list questions that students will be asked to consider in small groups.

Similarly, most classrooms used for discussion sections contain desks or tables and chairs that may be rearranged as instruction requires. The

TAs teach in a wide variety of environments. This Tai Chi class requires open space to facilitate freedom of movement.

authors of the University of California–Davis *TA Handbook* recommend that "*if you want lots of discussion,* place desks or chairs in a circle or horseshoe."[6] And, of course, they are right. Students are more likely to engage in discussion if they can see each other. When a room contains tables and chairs, a rectangular arrangement of furniture is possible. Whichever pattern (circle, horseshoe, rectangle) is used, TAs should expand the pattern to accommodate all students. Students who are seated outside any of these patterns will feel divorced from the interactive network. If several students are so situated, they may initiate a private conversation, engage in terrorist acts, or otherwise disrupt the class.

When approaching a classroom, TAs should ask themselves questions such as: What do I want to happen today? Will the customary physical environment be conducive to such activities? How might the physical environment be changed to improve the quality of instruction? Over the duration of a semester, it is unlikely that an identical physical setting will be appropriate for all of the activities that a TA has planned. Even in a rigid classroom setting with desks bolted to the floor in rows and columns, TAs may alter the environment by having students "stand to discuss issues in small groups (the cocktail party model), sit on the floor in the open spaces in the room, or form clusters with those on either side of them. . . . Students may have to straddle a desk, sit sideways, or turn their bodies a bit, but visual contact is possible."[7]

Kenneth Eble has noted that college "classroom conditions for teaching vary from superb to mediocre to awful, with adequate but uninspiring probably descriptive of most."[8] When assigned to a classroom that is less than ideal, given instructional goals and methods, TAs should not be reticent about asking for a room change. When a change is not possible, it is necessary to make the most of what one has. TAs may find some small solace in the realization that "the teacher is more important to what happens in the classroom than is the classroom itself."[9] Creative TAs are able to adapt classroom environments to their instructional purposes.

Attending to the Psychological Environment

Related to, but more important than, the physical environment is the psychological environment. In creating a supportive psychological climate, TAs may decenter themselves in the classroom, encourage student interaction, and reduce their perceived power advantage.

Decentering Oneself in the Classroom

Elizabeth Cohen has observed that teachers seem to prefer class structures in which they are clearly in charge. Seventy-five percent of the time, classrooms are so organized that only one whole-class communication network exists. Within that network, the instructor is the central figure as the primary initiator and target of classroom messages.[10]

Since the majority of professors TAs have known are very much at the psychological centers of their classrooms, it is only natural for TAs to take center stage in their own classrooms. While it is a natural impulse, it is in many cases unwise. TAs are often employed to have direct interaction with students in discussion, laboratory, or autonomous sections. It is expected that the central focus is on the student and his or her learning needs. TAs who seize the psychological center of their classrooms often misunderstand their function as TAs. The MIT guide stresses this point in the following way:

> A recitation without interaction—what problem could be more basic? Without the ease of communication that's supposed to be fostered by small groups, why have recitations at all? . . . It's bad for your students, who already have sat through many lectures and don't really want another one from you. They need a chance to talk and express themselves, to clarify their own thinking, to share their difficulties with each other, to experience the feeling of a group working together on mutual problems. This is what recitations are about, and getting it to happen in yours ought to be your number one priority.[11]

In many classroom settings the TA's primary function is either to encourage student interaction or to facilitate student learning. It is difficult to serve either of these functions from the psychological center of the classroom.

One means of decentering oneself psychologically in the classroom is to encourage interaction among students. In the beginning, TAs can encourage interaction by asking students to react to each others' responses to TA questions. As students gradually assume greater responsibility for the direction of a class discussion, TAs can reinforce this behavior through praise. In the long run, the decentered TA is working for a classroom environment in which students interact in an animated and spontaneous manner about relevant course content.

Encouraging Student Interaction

In order to encourage student interaction, TAs must relinquish some control of class proceedings. Whereas a rigidly led discussion may cut a straight path to the TA's objectives, a discussion with shared leadership may meander a bit and is likely to consume more time. Still, certain advantages accrue. Fuhrmann and Grasha have noted that such a communication pattern "encourages less dependence on the teacher, and students can thus take more initiative and responsibility. One result is that there is more involvement and interest on the part of students."[12]

Later in this chapter, specific strategies for increasing student involvement in classroom learning will be considered. Some of these strategies involve whole-class structures while others involve small-group activities.

Another means of decentering oneself psychologically is to reduce one's perceived power advantage. Students may be reluctant to participate in classroom activities and discussions because they are intimidated by the TA. Such students perceive their TAs as being more intelligent and powerful than they are; they fear that TAs will use this perceived power advantage to the detriment of their students.

Reducing One's Perceived Power Advantage

Fuhrmann and Grasha refer to this phenomenon as "psychological size" and note that when one party is seen as psychologically bigger than the other, open dialogue is likely to suffer.[13] They note that among the factors that may elevate an instructor's psychological size are using high status and titles, using sarcasm and ridicule, discouraging disagreement, using a formal manner, using punishing remarks, displaying vast knowledge, using complicated language, failing to use student names, and overemphasizing grades.[14]

TAs wishing to reduce their perceived power advantage—psychological size—may eliminate these factors from their own teaching.[15] Discrepancy in psychological size may also be reduced by elevating the psychological size of one's students.[16] Fuhrmann and Grasha offer the following advice for doing so:

> You can do this by exhibiting a genuine interest in what they have to say. Show some regard for their opinions, and give them a chance to talk. Let students see that they can influence you.[17]

TAs who demonstrate respect for their students find that their students tend to act in a manner that merits that respect.

Strategies for Encouraging Student Involvement

In addition to creating a supportive physical and psychological environment, TAs can encourage student involvement by using both whole-class and small-group strategies. These strategies may be used by TAs in lecture courses and in discussion, laboratory, and autonomous sections.

Using Whole-class Structures Creatively

Even when working with students in whole-class structures, TAs can increase the level of student participation. In this section, six strategies for doing so will be considered.

Student Summaries   Instead of summarizing a previous lecture, discussion, or laboratory period themselves and instead of providing their own summaries at the end of a period, TAs may ask students to do so. In this way, TAs share an important responsibility with students while encouraging them to pay careful attention to the content of lecture, discussion, and laboratory periods.

Student Reports   Rather than asking questions orally during class meetings, TAs may give questions to individual students at the end of preceding lecture or section meetings. The students who are given the questions may then present a more thoughtful response during the next period. This strategy is especially useful when dealing with difficult or complex materials. Student reports on recommended readings may also enrich and add variety to class meetings.

Debates   In all subject-matter fields, there are issues that students may debate. Rather than merely asking questions about issues, TAs may organize debates in which students are required to challenge each others' ideas. TAs need only phrase propositions (e.g., the Civil War was fought over a political issue rather than a moral issue), determine the debate format (i.e., number of speakers on each side, length of constructive and rebuttal speeches, acceptable audience responses), and choose speakers to speak for and against the proposition. Debates are valuable since they require students, both speakers and listeners, to think critically about major issues in a subject-matter field.

Panels   Student panels may be used for many different purposes. Panels may be formed so that student members role play major theorists discussing a common issue from varying perspectives. In literature courses, authors or characters may replace theorists. When students are reluctant to ask questions, a panel of students may be empowered as designated questioners for the day. A panel may also be formed to provide peer feedback when students are giving reports to the whole class. Students who are sent forth as a group to do research on a topic can often report their findings in the form of a panel discussion.

Brainstorming   At the beginning of a unit or project it is sometimes useful to brainstorm ideas. Brainstorming is designed to stimulate student thinking. Students are expected to produce as many ideas as they can. Two students may be appointed to record on the chalkboard as ideas are shouted out by their peers. By tradition, students are not permitted to be judgmental during a brainstorming session. TAs should ensure that evaluative comments are postponed for a later time. The brainstorming format permits students to get a sense of the broad range of ideas that are or may be related to a topic.

Simulations of Deliberative Groups   At times, TAs and their students may profit from simulating a decision-making group. Students in an international relations section might simulate the UN Security Council, with each student assigned to represent a member country. Students in education courses can simulate teaching. Students in a business ethics course might simulate an arbitration hearing to evaluate client grievances against an investment corporation. Simulations may involve deliberations from history, from present contexts, and even from the distant future. It is preferable to conduct simulations in small groups whenever possible since the smaller the group the greater the participation of each member. Still, there are times when whole-class simulations are the best means for accomplishing course objectives. Since many deliberative groups are large, attempts to simulate them in a fairly realistic manner will require that all of the students in the class participate.

There are two major alternatives to whole-class structures: individual study and small-group study. On occasion, students may spend time productively working alone with materials provided by instructors. On many

Using Small-group Structures Creatively

other occasions, students learn by interacting with one or more peers as they complete a learning task assigned by the TA. In the pages that follow, attention is given to the kinds of small-group activities that may serve as alternatives to traditional whole-class structures.

Small-group Discussions   Anything that can be talked about in a whole-class discussion can also be talked about in small groups. All the TA need do is announce a topic or question, write discussion questions on the chalkboard, or distribute a printed list of questions. Small-group discussions have two major advantages. First, it is probable that all students will participate in the small-group discussion. While reticent students often remain mute in a discussion involving fifteen to twenty people in a class or section, they will be less inhibited when talking to from one to four students. Second, small-group discussions enhance the quality of subsequent whole-class discussions. TAs often complain about how hard they have to work to get students involved in a whole-class discussion. They discover, however, that students who previously talked about questions in small groups are eager to share small-group conclusions with other students in the class.

Completion of Worksheets   In some courses, class time is often used for students to complete problem sets or worksheets. This is especially true in mathematics and in the sciences. While many TAs have their students work individually on problem sets or worksheets, it is more enjoyable for students if they are encouraged to work together in dyads and triads. Unfortunately, worksheets are used less frequently by discussion section TAs in the humanities and the social sciences. Many TAs seem to prefer to keep students in whole-class structures even though small-group interaction around worksheets would involve greater student participation and enjoyment. Almost all instruction at the cognitive levels of comprehension and application may involve student interaction about worksheet problems. Whatever the subject matter, TAs may prepare worksheets that require students to match concept labels with concept definitions (comprehension). Similarly, TAs across the subject-matter fields may provide lists of examples or specific instances of concepts for students to identify by type (application). Since application-level questions are difficult to ask, worksheets are often an easier and more appropriate method of teaching at this cognitive level.

Case Studies   Class meetings also may be devoted to the analysis or evaluation of cases or instances. While it is sometimes possible to perform case studies through whole-class discussions, it is not always possible or convenient to do so. For example, if sets of materials are limited it is probably best for students to be assigned to small groups with each group working with a different set of materials. As groups finish, the materials may be rotated around the classroom to other groups. Across a university curriculum, a wide variety of "cases" may be subjected to analysis and/or evaluation: literature, films, speeches, television programming, painting, sculpture, music, theories, models, diagnoses, and the list goes on. When undergraduates are encouraged to use information to analyze and evaluate cases, the intellectual level of courses is increased substantially.

Simulations   Simulations are synthesis-level activities through which students may role play behaviors that are not really available to them on campus. For example, students may simulate being tourists in a French restaurant, interviewing for a position in business or industry, being advertising executives in a New York City agency, or being the Japanese Naval High Command replanning naval strategies for World War II. Simulations are capable of bringing the entire world into the college classroom. Simulations are not bound by time or place. Simulations may be used in virtually any subject matter field. All that is required is a creative TA to encourage students to use information in imaginative ways.

The First Class Meeting

The first class meeting is especially important since students often use it as a barometer of course or section climate. Students take first impressions seriously. The MIT guide observes:

> The first day of class is important. "First impressions last." Some students seem to think the saying is "First impressions are the last"—they bolt out of their first-day recitation to the undergraduate office where they queue up to see what other section is open.[18]

TAs may productively use the first class day to clarify course expectations, to set the tone of the course, and to provide initial motivation.

Clarifying Course or Section Expectations

Like the MIT students mentioned, many undergraduates use the first class meeting as the basis for deciding whether they should add or drop the course. If students are to make intelligent decisions about courses and sections, TAs must provide necessary information about course expectations. The course or section syllabus or outline should be distributed at this time. Some TAs distribute a course or section fact sheet so that students may read as well as listen to course expectations.

In addition to providing basic course information, TAs should do whatever they think necessary to guide student decision making about course appropriateness. The Wisconsin manual urges TAs to do the following:

> Give students an idea of what your classroom style will be like and what to expect of the time they spend in class. For example, let them know whether you intend to spend most of the time solving problems, discussing case studies, quizzing them on lecture material, etc. Also let them know how you plan to structure the class activities—do you expect students to do most of the discussing of the material? Do you plan to have them work in groups? Should they be taking notes?[19]

A number of manuals urge TAs to work sample problems that students should be able to solve already or to indicate skills necessary for successful course performance.[20] There are no valid reasons for concealing course expectations. Neither TAs nor their students profit from students being enrolled in courses or sections for which they are ill-qualified or overqualified.

Setting the Tone of the Course or Section

The first class meeting may also set the tone of the course or section, which is indicated both by what the TA says and what the TA does. TAs who say they enjoy talking with students as they announce one office hour per week are unlikely to be convincing. TAs who announce four office hours a week, two of which are held in the union or student commons, are making quite a different statement.

The Berkeley handbook urges TAs to be especially careful to establish a classroom climate that is friendly and encouraging to *all* students. TAs are advised to be sensitive to subtle racism or sexism. It is suggested that TAs "make eye contact with minority as well as nonminority students after asking a question to invite a response," intervene if "male students pick up on each others' points but ignore an appropriate comment offered by a woman," and "discourage . . . offensive humor. . . ."[21]

TAs who take time during the first class meeting to introduce themselves and to invite students to do the same suggest to students that they wish to relate to them as real people. Similarly, TAs who invite students to express concerns and voice preferences about the course set a tone for mutual caring and respect.

TA enthusiasm for the subject matter, the course, and teaching in general strongly influences student attitudes toward a course or section. TAs should be sensitive to the motivational value of the first class period. The Wisconsin manual advises its readers to:

> make sure that you save time to actually start teaching. It's important to use the first day's flush of enthusiasm as effectively as possible to excite your students about the course. Don't dismiss the first class early—it can create a mistaken impression about your approach to the class. If students have not yet read or covered the material, use the time to point out what they should be paying attention to as they read; use the first assignment as an example for their future work in the course.[22]

The initial period should whet student appetites for the periods that follow, both in terms of course content and course pedagogy. It would be unwise for the TA to fill the first class period with "a long uninterrupted lecture: the message for today is that you want them to talk, too"[23]—both on the first day and throughout the term.

Motivating Students

TAs may demonstrate sensitivity to the quality of the classroom environment by recognizing and accepting responsibility for nonsupportive settings. TAs may then establish a supportive physical and psychological environment, employ whole-class structures that invite student participation, and use small-group activities that invite student interest and involvement. Finally, the first class meeting can start the course or section well by clarifying expectations, setting the tone, and motivating students.

Summary

Notes

1. Unnamed MIT undergraduate student, *The Torch or the Firehose? A Guide to Section Teaching* (Cambridge: Undergraduate Academic Support Office, Massachusetts Institute of Technology, 1981), p. 5.
2. Barbara Schneider Fuhrmann and Anthony F. Grasha, *A Practical Handbook for College Teachers* (Boston: Little, Brown and Company, 1983), p. 137. Used with permission.
3. Fuhrmann and Grasha, p. 137.
4. Fred I. Steele, *Physical Settings and Organization Development* (Reading, Mass.: Addison-Wesley, 1973), pp. 113–22.
5. Steele, p. 113.
6. *TA Handbook* (Davis: Teaching Resources Center, University of California–Davis, no date), p. 14. Emphasis in the original source.
7. Fuhrmann and Grasha, p. 147.
8. Kenneth E. Eble, *Professors as Teachers* (San Francisco: Jossey-Bass, 1972), p. 15.
9. Eble, p. 18.

10. Elizabeth G. Cohen, "Sociology and the Classroom: Setting the Conditions for Teacher–Student Interaction," *Review of Educational Research* 42 (1972): 441–52.

11. *The Torch or the Firehose?* p. 5.

12. Fuhrmann and Grasha, p. 143.

13. Fuhrmann and Grasha, p. 143.

14. Fuhrmann and Grasha, pp. 144–45.

15. Fuhrmann and Grasha, p. 145.

16. Fuhrmann and Grasha, p. 145.

17. Barbara Schneider Fuhrmann and Anthony F. Grasha, *A Practical Handbook for College Teachers* (Boston: Little, Brown and Company, 1983), pp. 145–46. Used with permission.

18. *The Torch or the Firehose?* p. 20.

19. *Manual for Teaching Assistants* (Madison: College of Letters and Science, University of Wisconsin–Madison, 1985), p. 11.

20. See, for example, *Manual for Teaching Assistants*, p. 10, and *The Torch or the Firehose?* p. 20.

21. *Learning to Teach: A Handbook for Teaching Assistants at U.C. Berkeley* (Berkeley: The Graduate Assembly, University of California–Berkeley, 1985), p. 55.

22. *Manual for Teaching Assistants*, p. 11.

23. *The Torch or the Firehose?* p. 21.

6

Lecturing

"To hear a good lecture is an inspiring experience. We leave with our imagination broadened and our interest piqued; we find ourselves entertained, prodded, and illuminated in turn. . . . Like a dramatic monologue, it engages our emotions and keeps them in play. . . . It mixes humor and erudition, and gives us a sense of the personal involvement of the lecturer in his or her topic."[1]

Heather Dubrow and
James Wilkinson
"The Theory and Practice
of Lectures"

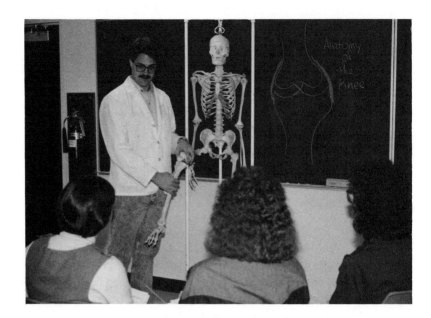

TAs in laboratory and discussion sections frequently give mini-lectures when explaining concepts.

As this quotation observes, a lecture can be an inspiring experience for students. It can prod, illuminate, entertain, and engage the emotions. Unfortunately, it can also bore, obfuscate, sedate, and cause frustration.

During their years of graduate study, TAs will wish to acquire the skills that effective lecturing requires. This is, however, not an easy task. While professors are expected to lecture a lot, TAs are not. In discussion, laboratory, and skill-development sections, TAs are expected to lead discussions and facilitate student work rather than lecture. As a consequence, TAs must seize opportunities to serve as guest lecturers for their supervisory professors and as appointed lecturers in intermediate-level courses. Since such opportunities are not available to everyone, TAs in traditional assignments should recognize that all TAs give mini-lectures when making assignments, explaining concepts, and demonstrating procedures. TAs who plan carefully for such mini-lectures, and who attend to matters of vocal and physical delivery and language use when implementing their plans, can acquire the skills they will need for full-fledged lecturing in the coming years.

This chapter will begin with a brief discussion of the values of lecturing. Attention will then be given to strategies for organizing ideas, making ideas interesting, and inviting class involvement.

Lecturing is an established element in college teaching. It is, in fact, the strategy of choice among college instructors. One survey of over 6,000 classes found that 24 percent were listed as "Lecture," 27 percent as "Lecture and Discussion," and 20 percent as "Lecture with Lab."[2]

The Values of Lecturing

Although the lecture was born in another age, when professors read from their notes because books were not generally available, it has survived the invention of the printing press,[3] the development of modern electronic technology, and even the contemporary notion that education is "a process of discovery in which the student is the main agent, not the teacher."[4] So why has the lecture survived as such a major force in university life? Three values of lecturing are apparent.

Since a lecture is a contemporary event, it can provide recent information that effectively supplements the material provided in the textbook(s) for the course. It can provide knowledge of the very latest findings gleaned from articles, convention presentations, and the instructor's own research.[5]

Provides New Information and Insights

The best lectures not only transmit information, they demonstrate obscure relationships, challenge conventional wisdom, introduce new modes of thought, and otherwise offer insights that go well beyond those provided by the printed text.[6] The best lecturers also adapt printed information to the needs and interests of their students by providing additional examples and showing the relevance of the information to those assembled.

Great lectures are inspiring performances. They begin with teacher/ scholars who are hopelessly in love with their subjects and who are obsessed with the notion that their students must come to share their love. This thought has been expressed by a number of authors in a variety of ways. Joseph Epstein, editor of a volume in praise of great teachers, concluded, "What all the great teachers appear to have in common is love of their subject [and] an obvious satisfaction in arousing this love in their students."[7] Philosopher Sidney Hook, writing in praise of Morris R. Cohen, his graduate school professor, notes that what makes a great teacher is "their manner and method, their enthusiasm and intellectual excitement, and their capacity to arouse delight in, and curiosity about, the subject taught."[8] This value of lecturing was summarized by William Cashin when he noted, "Lectures can communicate the intrinsic interest of the subject matter." They can "convey the speaker's enthusiasm in a way that no book or other media can. Enthusiasm stimulates interest and interested, stimulated people tend to learn more."[9]

Inspires Student Interest in the Subject

Serves as a Model of Scholarship

Time magazine, after drawing portraits of eight renowned professors in a 1966 cover story, noted that each demonstrated sound scholarship, each was convinced that their scholarship "has an irreversible relevance to life," and each believed that "insights, ideas, ways of thinking, [and] methods of inquiry are far more important to implant in young minds than any specific points of knowledge."[10] Through lecturing, professors offer a view of what it means to pursue knowledge.

TAs may also serve as models of what it means to be committed to a life of scholarship. Since undergraduate students are closer in age and interests to TAs than they are to professors, models that TAs provide are sometimes even more powerful than the models provided by senior scholars. Lecturers, at whatever stage of professional development, can model how scholars approach questions or problems that are considered important within a field of study.

Organizing Ideas

Clarke observes that "the prospect of preparing and presenting a lecture can give rise to a discomforting anxiety, particularly for the novice."[11] While he is correct, having a well-organized lecture outline can help the TA to keep that anxiety under control. Although the process of organizing ideas can be time consuming, it is worth the effort. Clarke also notes that "the feelings of satisfaction (and relief) that follow a successful presentation often match the intensity of the original anxiety."[12]

Developing a Skeletal Structure

Planning for a lecture usually begins with a topic to be addressed or a question to be answered. From this core topic or question, a list of main points for the lecture is generated. Taken collectively, these main points address all of the major elements associated with the topic. Each main point may, in turn, lead to a list of subpoints that must be addressed if the main point is to be understood. This list of main points and subpoints constitutes a skeletal structure or outline for the lecture. In other words, "Every lecture should represent one whole idea, clearly explained, within which a number of distinct parts, also clearly explained, work toward greater clarity of the whole idea."[13]

The list of main points and the supporting lists of subpoints usually reflect an identifiable pattern. For example, when describing a process, explicating a text, or examining a period in history, a sequential or chronological pattern is often reflected. When describing physical objects or phenomena, lectures often depict spatial relationships of the individual components. While various organizational patterns may be used, the important point is that a lecturer should so arrange ideas that the pattern provides an accurate, coherent, and discernible view of the central topic. If students are expected to record lecture notes in a well-organized way, instructors should present ideas in the same manner.

The nitty-gritty of a lecture rests with the verbal and audiovisual supporting materials that are used to elaborate the skeletal outline. While elaborative details could directly support the core topic, this is not a frequent event. In fact, elaborative details are seldom used in support of even main points. It is at the level of subpoints that elaborative details normally emerge. With complex topics, the level of subordination calling for elaboration may even be at the sub-subpoint level.

Verbal supporting materials may take a number of forms. A lecture may amplify ideas by providing examples or illustrations, citing statistics, offering comparisons, providing contrasts, citing quotations, defining, or enumerating related elements.[14] Such verbal supporting materials help students "both to understand and to remember."[15]

Audiovisual supporting materials also may serve to elaborate main and supporting points in a lecture. The verbal message may be accompanied by objects and models, photographs and slides, maps, charts, graphs, chalkboard illustrations, transparencies, audio and video recordings, and live demonstrations.[16] Each of these audiovisual materials can help lecturers elaborate and clarify their ideas. Many campuses have large and small multimedia classrooms that enable instructors to enrich their lectures by using varied instructional media.

One popular axiom of lecturing is that students learn best from instructors "who tell them where they are going in the beginning, where they are as they proceed, and where they've been when they arrive."[17] Such structural signposts are useful since they help students find paths through lectures.

Initial Partitions   The introduction to a lecture often includes a statement that previews or partitions the body of the lecture that is to follow. By informing students in advance about the major structural divisions of the lecture, the instructor enables students to perceive the general pattern of ideas and to recognize each part as it unfolds.

Transitions   Transitions are structural signposts within the body of the lecture. They are of three types. *Signal words,* such as first, second, third, next, furthermore, on the other hand, and finally, indicate the flow and relationship of ideas in a clear and efficient manner. *Rhetorical questions* serve both as a transition and as a means of inviting the interest of students: "Where do we go from here?" "Why does this problem continue to plague us?" "What else can we expect?" *Linking phrases* are powerful transitional devices that tie ideas together by looking both backward and forward: "Now that we understand the policy, let us begin to consider its consequences." "So that explains the procedure, but what advantages does it hold?"

Providing Elaborative Details

Creating Structural Signposts

Internal Summaries   Periodically, lecturers may pause to review the information that has been provided. Such reviews enable students to compare their own perceptions of what has been said with the instructor's perceptions.

Final Summaries   In concluding lectures, instructors often provide a final summary. Such summaries remind students of the main points that were covered and provide them with a sense of psychological closure for the lecture.

Making Ideas Interesting

The values of lecturing noted earlier are not universally reflected in college classrooms and lecture halls. A study group sponsored by the Carnegie Foundation reported that "the college teaching we observed was often uninspired"[18] and that lecture information was "passively received" by students with "little opportunity for positions to be clarified or ideas challenged."[19]

While "the lecture method is preferred by most professors,"[20] it is a most demanding means of instruction. It is difficult to sustain the attention of an audience for forty-five or fifty minutes when the attention span of college students is closer to fifteen or twenty minutes.[21] This discrepancy between lecture length and student attention span challenges instructors to make their ideas interesting and memorable.

Unfortunately, many college instructors refuse to accept the challenge. They believe that if they are knowledgeable in their fields, they have no obligation to be interesting—"All one needs to teach mathematics is knowledge of mathematics." While substance *is* absolutely essential to effective lecturing, substance alone will not capture and sustain student attention. Excellent lecturers not only have something to say, they say it well.

Perceive the Lecture as a Public Moment

It is important for instructors to perceive lectures, even those given in smaller classes, as public moments. Such moments call for careful intellectual and psychological preparation. Great lectures are seldom produced by instructors who stop by the classroom to chat for fifty minutes. Satterfield draws a distinction between lecturing and talking. Talking involves the spontaneous expression of thoughts with little advanced thought or reflection. Lecturing, however, calls for "something better than talk."[22] It calls for attention to matters of structure and support as suggested in the previous section, but it also calls for an attempt to energize one's ideas in order that they may interest and inspire the student audience.

TAs are often faced with the challenge of making technical or abstract material clear and interesting to their students. (Reprinted by permission of University of Wisconsin–Madison / News & Information Service.)

As a public moment, lecturing requires emotional as well as intellectual preparation. Joseph Lowman advises lecturers not to walk directly from their offices or meetings to the lectern. Rather, the outstanding professors he interviewed "typically set aside from five to thirty minutes beforehand to think about the ideas they are going to teach."[23] A few moments of solitude help lecturers to collect their thoughts and to prepare psychologically for the public moment.

A lecture has been irreverently defined as a means for getting information from the professor's notes to the student's notes without having it pass through the heads of either. Critics of lecturing "paint a dreary picture of the stodgy old pedant (or an uninspiring nervous young one) listlessly mumbling overly-long and obtuse sentences read from crumbling, yellowed (or freshly word-processed) notes."[24] As a public moment, a lecture is an event, not a collection of pages completed back in the instructor's office. Lectures will change as instructors and their plans confront the dynamics of the classroom.

In presenting lectures, instructors should demonstrate a "sense of communication." While this term is difficult to define, it is easy to recognize in the classroom. Rather than mumbling word for word over their notes, lecturers with a sense of communication use their notes easily and well. They speak extemporaneously from their outlines, sounding spontaneous even though they are well prepared. They establish eye contact

Demonstrate a Sense of Communication

frequently with students in all parts of the audience. They are sensitive to student feedback and respond appropriately. They engage in asides encouraged by student reactions, and they invent new examples when prepared examples fail. Their facial expressions show their enthusiasm for the subject matter and for teaching. They punctuate their lectures with gestures and purposeful movement. They resist the impulse to talk to the chalkboard or other visual aids, focusing attention instead on their students. And finally, their oral delivery is varied, dynamic, and so paced that students have no difficultly taking notes. Good lectures must be accurate, but they need not be dull.

Express Ideas in a Vivid and Tangible Manner

In addition to presenting ideas effectively through vocal and physical delivery, excellent lecturers express their ideas in a vivid and tangible manner. Peter Stern and Jean Yarbrough, writing in praise of their former teacher, Hannah Arendt, note that she had the ability "to make ideas come alive and seem important . . . to handle them in such a way that they evoked a vivid, tangible sense of reality."[25]

The ability to express ideas in a vivid and tangible manner depends on the effective use of language. Satterfield indicts academic language for being "notoriously bad . . . needlessly polysyllabic, turgidly involuted, and simply overabundant."[26] "It prefers the abstract to the concrete . . . [and] it does not offer images to the senses . . . it is soporific."[27]

To avoid these pitfalls of academic language, lecturers should try to express their thoughts in *clear language*. Big words should be avoided when small ones will do. For example, the expression "infallible integrity is the quintessence of all programmatic stategems" carries no more content than the homely phrase "honesty is the best policy," and the latter is certainly more clear.

Ideas also may be made vivid and tangible by relating them to the students' lives. Ideas become *personally relevant* to students when instructors build student names into their examples, indicate how the knowledge can affect or improve humankind, show relationships between the new information and previous knowledge, and relate the information to recent events reported in the news media.

Ideas also may be made interesting by using *vivid language*. Excellent lecturers choose language carefully, selecting words that evoke strong visual images. They use simile, metaphor, personification, hyperbole, and irony to express their ideas in a fresh and forceful manner. Lecturers need not be sleep-inducing.

Although lectures have been the primary form of college teaching "since the Middle Ages," they are increasingly under assault "by distinguished education panels" and also "by student protestors, learning theorists, faculty development consultants,"[28] and even lecturers themselves. For example, the Carnegie panel cited a math professor who "went so far as to say that if he had been introduced to mathematics in the kind of large, distracting lecture hall he himself was teaching in, he would never have continued to study the subject."[29] The Carnegie panel concluded, "We strongly urge . . . that the finest teachers should teach freshmen, and that undergraduate classes should be small enough for students to have lively intellectual interaction with teachers and fellow students."[30]

While lectures are not in peril as the central element in the undergraduate curriculum, concerned college instructors are searching for ways to make lectures, even those held in large lecture halls, more participatory.[31] In this final section attention will be given to strategies that can encourage students to be thinkers about, rather than mere recorders of, lecture information.

The easiest method for inviting class involvement is to communicate a willingness to answer questions. Students are far more likely to raise their hands if their questions are viewed as a contribution rather than as an interruption. Since some students are reluctant to ask questions in a large lecture hall, instructors also may demonstrate a willingness to answer questions before class, after class, or during office hours. One professor even has made it possible for students to phone in questions via his telephone answering machine. Physiologist Roosevelt Pardi of the University of Nebraska sometimes returns the calls, but he answers most of the questions in a short classroom report called "News from the Hotline."[32] As chapter 10 will observe, this strategy also may be used by TAs to get ongoing feedback about their teaching.

Another method of inviting class participation in a lecture is to ask specific questions. The response rate for this strategy is much greater than that for the traditional query, "Are there any questions?" To check on student comprehension, the lecturer can phrase questions that require students to define, describe, or give an example. Students can be called upon by name to answer such questions. If done from the beginning of the term, students will be motivated to think carefully about lecture content so that they will be able to answer when their names are called. Students should, of course, be called upon in a friendly or even jovial manner and should be let off the hook if they do not have an answer.

Inviting Class Involvement

Welcome Questions

Ask Specific Questions

Have Students Talk to Their Neighbors

In one large chemistry class, the professor pauses periodically and gives students a topic or question to discuss with those seated nearby. When the students have had sufficient time, the professor blows a whistle, elicits a response or two, and resumes the lecture. This strategy has a number of advantages:

> Without the mini-discussion segment, the teacher might not have known the gaps in student knowledge and gone ahead with the next lesson, which is most serious in sequential science courses. Moreover, with energy shifts students experience a variety of voices and a sense of shared responsibility for their learning.[33]

This strategy is useful not only in science courses but across the college curriculum.

Impersonate a Character

A final method of encouraging student involvement in a large lecture class is for the instructor to impersonate a character. Using this strategy, the lecturer adopts the persona of a theorist, the textbook author, or a literary, contemporary, or historical figure. The students are invited to ask questions of the character. For example, students might inquire of a Marx impersonator why a communist revolution occurred in Russia rather than in Great Britain, why the American middle class has little class consciousness, and when the Soviet state will wither away. This strategy can make a lecture session more invigorating both for the students and for the instructor.

Summary

Since most teaching assistantships do not call for lecturing as such, most TAs will have to acquire skills during mini-lectures used to make assignments, explain concepts, and demonstrate procedures. TAs may, of course, volunteer to give guest lectures for their supervising professors. Lecturing is the most popular instructional mode at the college level. It is a valuable tool for providing new information and insights, inspiring student interest in the subject, and providing models of scholars in action. Effective lecturers organize their ideas carefully by developing a skeletal structure, providing elaborative details, and creating structural signposts. Recognizing that the length of lectures exceeds the attention spans of most college students, effective lecturers also seek to make their ideas interesting by perceiving lectures as public moments, demonstrating a sense of communication, and expressing ideas in a vivid and tangible manner. Finally, recognizing that lectures often encourage student passivity, excellent lecturers invite class involvement by welcoming questions, asking specific questions, having students talk to their neighbors, and impersonating a character.

1. Heather Dubrow and James Wilkinson, "The Theory and Practice of Lectures," in *The Art and Craft of Teaching,* ed. Margaret Morganroth Gullette (Cambridge, Mass.: Harvard-Danforth Center for Teaching and Learning, 1982), p. 25.
2. William E. Cashin, "Improving Lectures," *Idea Paper* 14 (Center for Faculty Evaluation and Development, Kansas State University, September, 1985): 1.
3. Cashin, p. 1.
4. Mortimer J. Adler, *The Paideia Proposal: An Educational Manifesto* (New York: Macmillan, 1982), p. 23.
5. Cashin, p. 1.
6. Peter J. Frederick, "The Lively Lecture—8 Variations," *College Teaching* 34:2 (1984): 44.
7. Joseph Epstein, "Introduction," in *Masters: Portraits of Great Teachers* ed. Joseph Epstein (New York: Basic Books, 1981), p. xii.
8. Sidney Hook, "Morris R. Cohen—Fifty Years Later," in Epstein, p. 34.
9. Cashin, p. 1.
10. "To Profess with a Passion," *Time,* May 6, 1966, p. 83.
11. John H. Clarke, "Building a Lecture that Works," *College Teaching* 35:2 (1985): 56.
12. Clarke, p. 56.
13. Clarke, p. 56.
14. For a discussion of verbal supporting materials see, for example, R. R. Allen and Ray E. McKerrow, *The Pragmatics of Public Communication*, 3d ed. (Dubuque, Iowa: Kendall/Hunt Publishing, 1985), pp. 62–74.
15. Cashin, p. 2.
16. For a discussion of visual and audio supporting materials see, for example, Allen and McKerrow, pp. 119–29.
17. Clarke, p. 56.
18. Ernest L. Boyer, *College: The Undergraduate Experience in America* (New York: Harper and Row, 1987), p. 151.
19. Boyer, pp. 149–50.
20. Boyer, p. 149.
21. Frederick, p. 44.
22. John Satterfield, "Lecturing," in Ohmer Milton and Associates, *On College Teaching* (San Francisco: Jossey-Bass, 1978), p. 41.
23. Joseph Lowman, *Mastering the Techniques of Teaching* (San Francisco: Jossey-Bass, 1984), p. 91.
24. Frederick, p. 44.
25. Peter Stern and Jean Yarbrough, "Hannah Arendt," in Epstein, p. 192.
26. Satterfield, p. 48.
27. Satterfield, p. 48.
28. Frederick, p. 43.
29. Boyer, p. 149.
30. Boyer, p. 149.
31. Frederick, for example, pp. 43–50, identifies eight varieties of the lecture, most of which would lead to increased student participation.
32. "Professor on Call," *Newsweek on Campus,* December 1985/January 1986, p. 6.
33. Frederick, p. 47.

7

Leading Class Discussions

"We need, first of all, to acknowledge our fears in facing discussion classes: the terror of silences, the related challenges of the shy and dominant student, the overly-long dialogue between ourself and one combative student, the problems of digression and transitions, student fear of criticism, and our own fear of having to say 'I don't know.' Worst of all, perhaps, is the embarrassment of realizing usually in retrospect that 'about half way through the period I lapsed, again, into lecture.' "[1]

Peter Frederick
"The Dreaded Discussion:
10 Ways to Start"

The effectiveness of class discussions may be judged against two criteria: How well does the discussion meet the individual needs of students, and how well does the discussion promote active student involvement? Since these criteria are difficult to meet in large lecture sessions, they become the responsibility of TAs in individual discussion sections.

Satisfying these criteria is not easy in discussion sections either. The Stanford TA handbook notes that "although sections are often delegated to the least experienced instructors, leading a discussion section is probably the most difficult because, unlike lectures, they may not be totally planned in advance."[2] TAs must adapt to unexpected happenings and must deal with student feelings as well as student intellectual concerns. It is much more difficult to interact *with* students than it is to lecture *to* students. Small wonder that Peter Frederick, author of the opening quotation, notes the fear and terror that instructors feel when approaching discussion classes.

A number of insights and skills required of discussion section TAs are considered in this chapter. It should become apparent that being a discussion section TA is an emotionally and intellectually challenging activity. It should also become apparent that much of the information presented in this chapter applies as well to discussions that occur in labs, autonomous sections, and other formats.

Determining the Function of Class Discussions

Discussion sections are referred to in a number of ways and serve a variety of functions. While "discussion section" is the term often used, such sections are also frequently referred to as review sections and recitation sections. In some cases, the terms discussion, review, and recitation sections are used to refer to the same phenomenon. In other cases, the terms are meant to denote different group functions. For example, at Stanford University both discussion sections and review sections are offered. In review sections, TAs have "about forty-five minutes to go over material covered in three or four fifty-minute lectures."[3] TAs are expected to highlight important concepts and review significant details. In these cases, the TA's behavior will "be closer to that of a lecturer than a discussion leader."[4] Similarly, the Mathematics Department at the University of Wisconsin–Madison provides both discussion sections and recitation sections. While TAs in discussion sections of lecture courses are expected to explain and extend material presented in lectures, TAs in recitation sections of lecture courses are expected to oversee the work of students as they "solve problems at the board either individually or in small groups."[5] When TAs oversee student work in recitation sections, they will employ strategies of the kind discussed in chapter 8, "Facilitating Student Learning."

Given that the purpose of the discussion section, whatever it is called, is to explain and extend information presented in lecture, it is necessary for the TA to determine the precise purpose or purposes of discussion on a given day. Among the functions that may be served by discussion sections are those that follow.

One of the major functions of a discussion section is to ensure that students have an accurate, complete, and unified view of the material covered in lecture. Often, TAs begin a discussion section either by providing a brief summary of the lecture or by asking a student to do so. TAs also frequently ask a series of questions that will force the students to demonstrate that they comprehend lecture content. The form and sequence of questions will be considered later in this chapter.

Clarify Lecture Content

The function of a discussion section meeting is often suggested by the content of the preceding lecture. For example, if the previous lecture was highly theoretical, the discussion section should probably be devoted to clarifying lecture content through the presentation of examples, definitions, restatements, and other kinds of expository materials. In some cases, abstract concepts may be made somewhat more concrete by a TA's attempt to represent them through a schema drawn on the chalkboard. In other cases, when a lecture has dealt with abundant detail, the discussion section should probably present the overall concept or theory around which the bits and pieces may be organized and understood.

Complement Lecture Content

The content of lectures normally functions at the recall and comprehension levels of the cognitive hierarchy. If the objectives of a course call for students to apply knowledge or use it in analysis-, synthesis-, and evaluation-level activities, such instruction will, most likely, take place in the discussion section. Even if the course director is content if students merely recall and comprehend information, TAs may still wish to encourage students to apply information appropriately. Information that is not used is soon forgotten. A number of vehicles for experiential learning are considered later in this chapter.

Apply Lecture Content

TAs, in discussion and laboratory sections, in autonomous sections, and in other instructional settings are often expected to clarify and extend material encountered by students in reading assignments. TAs normally review the major concepts presented in the reading, check student comprehension of the concepts, and invite students to apply the knowledge where appropriate.

Clarify and Extend Reading Assignments

Clarify Assignments

As students are introduced to a project or experiment, TAs often initiate a discussion about expectations or procedures. Lab TAs lead discussions about upcoming experiments in the manual or about replicating an experiment they have demonstrated. TAs in discussion sections and autonomous sections talk about expectations for upcoming assignments and invite student questions and ideas.

Evaluate Student Plans, Progress, Products, and Performances

As students pursue independent or small-group projects or experiments, TAs may pause periodically to talk about student work: Do the students have sound plans for their work? Are the students making adequate progress in their work? Are the outcomes of student work of desired quality? In skills courses in language, composition, speech communication, mathematics, art, and music, a good deal of attention is given to the discussion of student work.

Encouraging Student Participation

Chapter 5 considered strategies for encouraging student participation across class formats. This section considers strategies for increasing student involvement in class discussions.

Don't Be a Traffic Cop

Some discussion section TAs lead a class discussion like a traffic officer directs traffic. They establish eye contact with a person, provide a signal (in this case a question), secure a response, and repeat the process over and over again with other students. When TAs behave in this manner, there is little opportunity for genuine interaction to occur. One way to break this pattern is to invite students to react to each others' responses. This will get students in the habit of talking to each other about course content.

Provide Think Time

After asking a question and before calling on a respondent, it is helpful to provide a few seconds so that all students in the section can formulate a response. The amount of think time provided will vary, of course, with the level of difficulty of the question. By withholding the respondent's name until the very end of the think time, TAs ensure that all students will attempt to formulate a response.[6]

Don't Require Students to Raise Their Hands before Speaking

Most discussion sections are sufficiently small that it is not necessary for students to be recognized before speaking. If students are seated in a circle, horseshoe, or rectangle, they will be able to see each other and will not interrupt when someone else is speaking. It is difficult to have a spirited discussion when participants have to seek the TA's permission before speaking.

One of the quickest ways to stifle a discussion is to belittle student questions or to require students to rephrase questions that are ambiguous. Sometimes insecure TAs try to assert their intelligence by being sarcastic when responding to student questions; for example, "I thought I just answered that question!" or "Is that really relevant?" One more enlightened TA begins each term by announcing to his students that he has never met a question he didn't like. Students in his sections know that they will never be ridiculed for asking a "dumb" question.

Don't Belittle Student Questions

The authors of the Stanford guide urge instructors to "positively reinforce all responses whether correct or incorrect." In so doing, they allege, TAs will "create a safe environment for students to speak out and try new ideas."[7] While the intent of this recommendation is laudable, some TAs may not feel comfortable responding to inane answers by saying "That's interesting" or "good point!" So what is one to do? When a student responds in a less than accurate or sophisticated manner, TAs can simply offer no comment and invite other student responses.

Don't Belittle Student Responses

TAs sometimes get involved in "conversations" with a single student who, out of combativeness or curiosity, wishes to pursue a topic at length. When TAs are sidetracked from the mainline discussion in this way, a good deal of time is wasted for the remaining class members who are disinterested in the special topic. When students wish to plead special interests or probe a point in depth, they should be invited to stay after class or stop by during office hours.

Don't Get Sidetracked by Individual Students

As the opening quotation to this chapter suggests, it is easy for a TA discussion leader to lapse into lecturing without being aware of it. An uncontrolled response to a student question can consume valuable time that could have been spent exploring a range of questions and student concerns. Lapsing into lecture is the greatest single obstacle to student participation. Discussion sections should complement lectures rather than mirror them.

Don't Lapse into Lecture

Even exceptionally well-prepared and intelligent TAs will encounter student questions that they can't answer on the spot. When this occurs, TAs should simply admit that they don't have the answer. If desirable, the question may be answered at the next class meeting. If TAs frequently encounter questions they cannot answer, they should spend more time reviewing lecture and reading materials in advance of the discussion.

Don't Fake a Response

TAs use small group activities to increase student involvement and interest.

Don't Keep Students in Whole-class Structures Consistently

When the discussion involves the whole class, many students can avoid participating by being silent. TAs will sometimes conclude that "we really had an animated discussion" when, in fact, fewer than 50 percent of the section members said anything and 80 percent of the comments were made by three people—the TA and two students. When students are placed in small groups, it is very difficult for them to remain silent. After students consider questions in small groups, the TA may lead a whole-class discussion about the same questions. The discussion that results is likely to be more spirited than if the small-group discussions had not occurred.

Phrasing and Sequencing Questions

There are two types of questions: closed questions and open-ended questions. Closed questions call for relatively brief, right or wrong type responses: for example, "In what year did the French evacuate their forces from Vietnam?" Open-ended questions call for an elaborated response and often involve multiple acceptable answers: for example, "How is United States involvement in Nicaragua similar to and different from United States involvement in Vietnam?"

Just as it is possible to use the cognitive hierarchy[8] to write objectives and to stimulate the development of learning activities (see chapter

4), it is also possible to write discussion questions that function at several cognitive levels. For example, consider the following sequence of questions:

Recall: What are the six levels in Bloom's taxonomy in the cognitive domain?

Comprehension: How do you differentiate between recall and comprehension (or comprehension and application, or analysis and evaluation)?

Application: If I were to ask you to give me an example of a recall-level objective, at what cognitive level would my question be functioning?

Analysis: What cognitive levels are likely to be represented in the objectives of a chemistry course that includes a laboratory section?

Synthesis: Who can invent a series of objectives for an area of content that reflects the recall through synthesis cognitive levels?

Evaluation: It is claimed that each level of the cognitive hierarchy assumes the previous cognitive levels. What arguments may be advanced to deny this allegation?

Although it doesn't make sense to drag all subject matter, kicking and screaming, up the cognitive ladder, the point should be clear: TA questions can increase or decrease the intellectual level of a class discussion. Discussions that merely invite student recall and probe student comprehension do not exploit the full potential of the discussion method. In an effective discussion, "the leader guides, challenges, and prods students to help them deal with issues."[9] The leader does not just ask for factual recall—he or she extends student thinking about course concepts or issues.

Providing for Task Roles in Discussions

Whether discussions occur in whole-class structures or small-group structures, certain task roles must be accomplished. In whole-class structures the TA is ultimately responsible for ensuring that these task roles are served. TAs may, of course, delegate reponsibilities to students. When students in discussion sections are placed in small discussion groups, TAs must ensure that students in the group are serving these task roles. Among the task roles that may be identified are those that follow.[10]

Initiator (Energizer)

In any discussion, someone must get things started. In whole-class discussions it is normally the TA who serves this role. When TAs do not serve this role well, discussions are slow to start. It seems to take some

TAs forever to take attendance, make announcements, hand back homework, and preview the period. Sometimes TAs take ten to fifteen minutes just getting things started. Competent TA initiators are well into section activities five minutes after the beginning of class.

TAs who encourage students to work in small groups must ensure that someone in the group assumes the initiator role. After placing students in groups, the TA should move rapidly around the room to learn whether students have begun the desired learning task. When students are still getting organized, the TA may facilitate small-group interaction by role playing initiator: "OK, let's get cracking" or "What are we trying to do here?"

**Task Clarifier
(Direction Finder)**

In whole-class as well as small-group discussions, someone must clarify the task of the group. In whole-class discussions, the TA normally previews what will occur during the discussion. When students are unsure about the task or the direction of the interaction, they may seek clarification by asking the TA questions.

When students are assigned to small discussion groups within a discussion, lab, or autonomous section, someone within the group must provide leadership in clarifying the task or pointing the direction for group interaction. When it is apparent that no one has assumed this leadership role in a student learning group, the TA may model the role of the task clarifier by asking, "What final product is your group trying to produce?" or "Why am I asking you to engage in this discussion?"

**Questioner
(Direction Giver)**

In any discussion group, someone must ask questions and provide the general direction for group interactions. In whole-class discussions, the TA is expected to provide the general directions that students need in order to behave in a competent manner. In upper-division courses, instructors often are happy to share this task role with students.

When students are working in a small group, one or more of them must provide direction for the group through careful questioning. Since students are reluctant to command each other ("Do it this way!") or even to suggest to each other ("Let's do it this way"), directions normally take the interrogative form ("Why don't we try it this way?" or "What else should we add to this section?").

Secretary (Recorder)

In whole-class discussions, students are their own secretaries—taking notes as the discussion unfolds. When students work in small groups, however, one person normally assumes the secretarial role to ensure that the group is preparing a single response or product. On many occasions, the person who records group progress also actively contributes to the group through other task roles.

At some point, in both whole-class and small-group discussions, someone should ask questions about or make comments on the quality of questions, answers, examples, and lists or other products. In whole-class discussions, the TA normally serves this role. As students mature, however, they become more willing to make critical comments about their own work, the work of others, and even the work of the TA. Competent and confident TAs can cope with and learn from student evaluations (see chapter 10).

Evaluator (Critic)

In small-group discussions, students must serve the evaluative role for themselves. Since small groups often report their findings or share their products with the whole class, individuals within the small groups should do their best to ensure that their work is of good quality.

A person who plays this task role informs others of group progress and reminds others of work yet to be done. In whole-class discussions, a summary is not likely to occur unless the TA provides one or asks students to provide one.

Summarizer (Orienter)

In small-group discussions, students can be encouraged to provide a summary or orientation if the TA builds such a component into the assignment given to the group. When student small groups are ongoing in nature, the importance of periodic summary and orientation is magnified.

The importance of affect in learning has been noted elsewhere. In discussion sections, as in all other learning environments, college students should have positive feelings about the learning experience. Social–emotional roles consist of those tasks that cause learners to feel good about their membership and achievement in learning groups. Among the social–emotional roles that may be served by TAs and students are those that follow.[11]

Providing for Social–Emotional Roles in Discussions

The encourager tries to get others involved in the discussion. In whole-class discussions, most TAs try to democratize discussions by calling on students who have not participated previously in the discussion and by asking students to comment on the ideas of other students. TAs who encourage widespread student participation can avoid domination of the discussion by one or a few students. If the TA role plays encourager effectively, students in small-group discussions may do the same. Statements of encouragement often sound like the following: "How do you feel about this issue, Dave?" or "Didn't you do a paper on this topic, JoAnne?"

Encourager

Supporter	Persons who assume the supporter role praise people for their performances: "That's a great idea; tell us more." "Now I think we're on the right track; good job." In whole-class discussions, TA responses to student answers or work samples should not be too effusive. If a TA reacts with "super" to everything students contribute, the word super rapidly becomes mediocre. When students are assigned to work together in small groups, they should be encouraged to react positively to the worthwhile contributions of their peers.
Harmonizer	While controversy in the classroom can be a constructive force, it can also get in the way of learning. When tempers flare in a whole-class discussion, the TA must step in to encourage cooler heads to prevail. While argument is at the heart of the academic experience, standards of enlightened advocacy must be maintained. When college students engage in small-group discussions, they must police their own disputes. Abusive behaviors should not be tolerated in small-group discussions any more than they are in whole-class discussions ("Now, wait a minute! You people don't have to agree, but at least give each other a chance to finish an argument.").
Cheerleaders	Cheerleaders incite enthusiasm for the task. They are confident that their groups can accomplish any task. TAs who serve the cheerleader role tend to be well liked by their students since they treat them with affection and respect ("This is a tough assignment, but I'm confident that you guys can do it."). In small-group discussions, students must serve as cheerleaders for each other ("C'mon, we can handle this!"). When small groups are assigned competitive tasks in discussion sections, cheerleaders will emerge naturally.
Compromiser	When students engage in enlightened advocacy (see harmonizer), they may nonetheless reach an impasse. College students who play by the rules still come to differing conclusions. When students in a whole-class discussion are firmly committed to opposite positions on an issue, the TA should encourage class members to find a midpoint ("Both of these points of view are worthy of consideration. Is there a middle ground?"). In preparing students for small-group discussions, TAs should inform them about the nature and importance of group consensus. When two students in a small group are locked in controversy, it becomes the responsibility of another member of the small group to serve as compromiser.

It is important that TAs be sensitive to their students' feelings. Since feelings influence learning, both positively and negatively, TAs should try to ensure that students are in the proper frame of mind. Empathic TAs need two kinds of skills: they must be able to determine a student's emotional state by interpreting verbal and nonverbal signs of feelings, and they must provide an opportunity for students to express feelings. In a whole-class discussion, for example, the TA may simply query, "You seem intrigued by my suggestion, Sally. Do you really think it will work?" In small-group discussions, the students will have to attend to their own feelings. Through role modeling and through direct suggestion, TAs can encourage students to be aware of and to respond appropriately to the feelings of their peers.

Feeling Finder

Summary

A major responsibility of TAs is to lead class discussions. Class discussions serve a number of valuable functions. They can clarify lecture content, complement lecture content, apply lecture content, clarify and extend reading assignments, clarify assignments, and evaluate student plans, progress, products, and performances. In leading effective class discussions, the TA should avoid being a traffic cop, provide think time, not require students to raise their hands before speaking, not belittle student questions, not belittle student responses, not get sidetracked by

When leading whole-class discussions, the TA sets both the intellectual and the social climate of the classroom.

individual students, not lapse into lecture, not fake a response, and not keep students in whole-class structures consistently. TAs can influence the intellectual level of class discussions by learning to phrase questions at differing cognitive levels. Finally, when leading class discussions, TAs should be sensitive to the task roles and social–emotional roles that are being served either by self or by students in the class. When important roles are being neglected, the TA may serve these roles or invite students to do so.

Notes

1. Peter Frederick, "The Dreaded Discussion: 10 Ways to Start," *Improving College and University Teaching* 29:3 (Summer 1981): 109.
2. Michele Fisher, ed., *Teaching at Stanford: An Introductory Handbook,* rev. ed. (Stanford, Calif.: Center for Teaching and Learning, Stanford University, 1983), p. 11.
3. Fisher, p. 14.
4. Fisher, p. 15.
5. "Helpful Hints to Good Teaching," unpublished manuscript (Madison: Department of Mathematics, University of Wisconsin–Madison, 1983), pp. 8–9.
6. *A Handbook for University of Michigan Teaching Assistants* (Ann Arbor: Center for Research on Learning and Teaching, 1983), p. 18.
7. Fisher, p. 13.
8. Benjamin S. Bloom, Mac D. Englehart, Edward J. Furst, Walter H. Hill, and David R. Krathwohl, *Taxonomy of Educational Objectives—The Classification of Educational Goals, Handbook I: Cognitive Domain* (New York: David McKay Company, 1956).
9. Kenneth E. Hoover, *College Teaching Today: A Handbook for Postsecondary Instruction* (Boston: Allyn and Bacon, 1980), p. 123.
10. This list is based on the work reported by Kenneth D. Benne and Paul Sheats, "Functional Roles of Group Members," in *Small Group Discussion: A Reader,* 2d ed., eds. Robert S. Cathcart and Larry A. Samovar (Dubuque, Iowa: William C. Brown, 1974), pp. 181–82.
11. Cathcart and Samovar, pp. 182–83.

8

Facilitating Student Learning

"We have seen instructors attempt teaching methods such as lecturing only because they were taught that way. They are not particularly good at lecturing, yet they persist. One response they give us for their behavior is 'I really don't know any other ways that would be more effective.' The goals and values inherent in such approaches are not selected after a careful consideration and testing of alternatives. They are adopted simply because they are handy."[1]

Barbara Schneider Fuhrmann
and Anthony Grasha
A Practical Handbook for
College Teachers

Fuhrmann and Grasha note that some college instructors do not select teaching strategies in a thoughtful manner; rather, they simply teach as they were taught, whether or not the strategy is consistent with their talents, goals, and values or the circumstances in which they find themselves. Like other college instructors, some TAs also enter into the act of teaching in a less than thoughtful manner. They do not stop to ask themselves questions such as: Why is this course taught in small autonomous sections? Why have I been assigned to work with students in one-on-one contexts? Why are laboratory sections necessary in this course? Many universities employ TAs to facilitate student learning or progress in various contexts—as instructors in skill-development courses; as coaches, tutors, supervisors, and advisors; and as directors of laboratory sections. In all of these situations, TAs are responsible for facilitating student learning and for bridging the gap between theory and application.

TAs who are employed to facilitate student learning will fail egregiously if they misinterpret their function. They are not employed to lecture, to lead esoteric discussions, or to utter authoritative pronouncements. Rather, facilitators are employed to guide, help, and encourage students as they seek to acquire subject-matter competence and skill. In this chapter, three types of facilitative TA appointments will be examined.

Teaching Autonomous Sections

TAs often find themselves appointed as leaders of one or more autonomous sections of a course directed by a regular faculty member. This model is frequently employed in such courses as public speaking, foreign language, physical education, art, music, and composition.

TAs in these situations should remember that they may or may not have complete autonomy. A course director may be in charge of fifteen or more TAs with thirty or more autonomous sections. Authoritarian course directors maintain strong control over the content and execution of their courses. Libertarian course directors allow TAs to be on their own. Democratic course directors offer the instructional staff the opportunity to engage in collective decision making regarding textbook selection, exam preparation, and classroom activities. When relating to such professors, TAs should not try to lead a revolution against authoritarians, should not be lackadaisical with libertarians, and should not be nonparticipatory with democrats.

TAs in charge of autonomous sections should keep in mind that the purpose of such sections is to provide direct interaction between students and the instructor in order to facilitate student skill development. TAs in such classes should resist the temptation to lecture extensively; to do so denies the very purpose of the classroom arrangement. It is also an inefficient use of resources since lectures can be delivered to a throng of 300 as easily as to a gathering of 15 to 30. Rather than lecturing, TAs should consider assuming either the student-centered or the process-centered approach to instruction.

TAs who teach autonomous sections out of a student-centered or holistic approach sometimes offer their students a potpourri of course options; students are permitted to choose one project from column A, one project from column B, and two projects, perhaps, from columns C and D. Even when all students are required to complete the same assignments, TAs encourage students to set personal goals for each project and to develop a personal learning schedule. Such TAs provide instruction when students need it or ask for it. With this approach students learn to write by writing, learn to dance by dancing, learn to swim by swimming, and learn to make films by filmmaking.

The Student-centered Approach to Autonomous Sections

TAs directing autonomous sections out of a student-centered approach often act as "coaches." The "coach" relationship with students is far different from the "instructor" relationship. Instead of maintaining a distance between teacher and student (physically, emotionally, and intellectually), the coach creates an atmosphere of camaraderie. "Instructors" may not take Ds and Fs personally (although perhaps they should); "coaches" view deficient student performances as an indication of personal failure.

TAs who teach autonomous sections out of a process-centered approach normally provide a carefully prescribed sequence of instruction. Among the elements of instruction sometimes included in the sequence are precepts, examples, performance experiences, and evaluations.

The Process-centered Approach to Autonomous Sections

Precepts Precepts are simply principles, theories, or concepts that provide the intellectual basis for an area of study. They provide the information that students will need in order to develop performance competence.

Public speaking TAs can provide a set of precepts, originating with Plato, Aristotle, and Socrates, regarding the nature of effective oral communication in public contexts. Foreign language TAs can offer precepts concerning the form and function of linguistic units. A syllabus for an introductory course in swimming offered the following list of course precepts:

A. Principles of buoyancy
  1. Archimedes' principle
  2. Positive and negative buoyancy
  3. Specific gravity–density
  4. Physiological make-up of the body as related to swimming (vital capacity–body composition: fatty tissue, muscle, bone)
B. Balance
  1. Relationship of center of gravity and center of buoyancy
  2. Stable, unstable, and neutral equilibrium
C. Force production
  1. Body position as related to the skill
  2. Tension–relaxation
  3. Hydrodynamic lift force
  4. Resistance (profile, wave, skin)
  5. Newton's Laws of Motion
D. Physiology of gaseous exchange in the lungs particularly as it relates to breath control and hyperventilation[2]

Precepts provide the basis for skill learning. They are the foundation upon which process-centered instruction is based.

Examples   Process-centered approaches to instruction also use examples liberally. While the "coach" is likely to jump into the pool to demonstrate the desired skill, process-centered TAs are more likely to show the class instances of art, literature, discourse, or dance, or show samples of student work from a previous semester, or show videotapes of students demonstrating the skill. Public speaking TAs, for example, need not actually give speeches in class themselves, but they should require students to analyze speeches to see how the precepts apply. Examples of excellent compositions from prior semesters enable English TAs to clarify expectations and motivate students to excel in their own compositions.

Performance Experiences   In all skill development, there is no substitute for experience or practice. Instead of simply being told about a skill, students need to *do* it as well. Students in public speaking classes, for example, can be provided with a myriad of speaking activities requiring them to use various elements of delivery, patterns of organization, figures of speech, arguments, forms of proof, and the like. Eventually these layers of skills will find their way into speeches—each one with higher expectations than the last. Foreign language TAs also have no shortage of available activities, including drilling, oral quizzing, simulated conversation, and language laboratories. The aforementioned swimming class syllabus suggests the following list of activities to be mastered by the end of the semester: underwater breathholding, rhythmic breathing, basic floating on front and on back, prone glide with flutter kick, back glide with flutter kick, jumping in both shallow and deep water, survival floating, treading water, underwater swimming, and sculling on back.[3]

Evaluations   The final component of the process-centered model usually involves providing evaluative feedback regarding student learning. In providing evaluative feedback, TAs should judge the status of student performances and should provide emotional support, praise, and encouragement. Students in skill-development courses must receive honest feedback concerning their performances. They should also be praised and encouraged, however, so that they are motivated to continue to grow and improve.

Teaching Individuals

TAs also facilitate student learning by working with students individually as tutors and as writing consultants; as coaches in individual athletic, music, drama, art, and forensic events; and as supervisors and undergraduate advisors. In all of these contexts, TAs are expected to be in close personal contact with individual students.

Serving as Tutor

Graduate students, in search of financial gain, sometimes agree to tutor undergraduate students having difficulty in departmental courses. This is a legitimate thing to do. TAs also act as tutors for their own students during office hours. In either case, graduate students/TAs should serve as question askers rather than answer givers. Instead of providing precepts, tutors should engage in careful questioning to assist students in generating their own principles. The process of intellectual discovery in an academic discipline can be modeled by the TA serving as questioner.

Tutoring may be perceived as a process of "guiding students to discover."[4] Discovery may take place either through inductive or deductive inquiry. In the inductive mode, students are asked to observe examples, infer relationships, and state rules or generalizations.[5] In the deductive mode, students are asked to recall a rule or generalization, observe an instance or instances of the phenomenon generalized about, and affirm or deny the rule or generalization.[6] It is important to note that "discovery requires . . . the teacher [to] *assist* and *guide* the student as he does, discovers and learns from his experience. Both the teacher and the student are actively involved in the learning process."[7]

One of the major problems undergraduate students experience is learning to think and talk in the language of a discipline. A University of Washington genetics teaching assistant, Deborah Kranzler, observes: "When students come to me for help, I'm trying to get them to think not only *about* genetics, but *in* genetics."[8] The secret to effective tutoring is learning to empathize with the problems and frustrations of students, learning to provide an intellectual framework within which students may function, and learning to guide student thinking through careful questioning.

Serving as Writing Consultant

English departments nationwide employ graduate students as instructors or consultants in writing laboratories. There are great variations in the ways TAs are expected to function as writing lab consultants. In some cases students experiencing writing difficulty are expected to bring a writing sample to the first meeting with the consultant. The TA analyzes the sample, explains writing problems to the student, and sends the student forth to revise and edit prior to a follow-up conference.

In other labs TAs attempt to improve student writing skills by focusing on the writing process. During the first meeting the TA asks the student about potential topics and, through questioning, helps him or her to choose and narrow a topic. The TA also helps the student brainstorm ideas related to the topic and identify possible sources of information—again through questioning. At a second meeting the student reports progress to the TA and discusses possible ways of organizing the paper. The TA again asks probing questions and sends the student forth to write a draft. During the third meeting the TA provides feedback regarding the content of the paper through questioning; identifies problems in spelling, syntax, and punctuation; edits a sample paragraph to eliminate the problem; and sends the student forward to revise and edit. This process continues until the student paper is of acceptable quality.

In still other writing labs, students are assigned to a small group of cohorts who interact with each other during the writing process by asking questions, offering suggestions, and providing support for each other as the writing process unfolds. Cohort groups can also engage in peer editing as a means of assisting each other. When using such peer groups, the writing lab TA need only look in on the group periodically, offer encouragement to the group, provide instruction when they request it, and check final drafts of compositions to ensure that the students are writing well.

Some TAs are expected to
serve as coaches for
individual students.

Whatever system is employed by the writing lab TA, the teaching
is not successful unless permanent improvements in student writing occur.
Simply editing the student's paper will not solve the long-term problem
that brought the student to the writing laboratory in the first place.

Serving as Coach

TAs also work with students in one-on-one situations as coaches of athletic, music, drama, art, and forensic events. The student-centered approach to instruction is normally used in these situations.

While there are precepts for athletic, artistic, and intellectual skills,
TAs are not likely to teach them directly when working with students in
one-on-one contexts. Rather, the precepts will be taught informally when
the student needs them to advance in performance skills.

Coaches often provide personal demonstrations and examples. Art
instructors can show students their own sculptures, paintings, drawings,
and glassblowings, as well as those of the masters, and can demonstrate
specific techniques. Athletic coaches can offer demonstrations of specific
skills (shooting free throws, kicking field goals, or hitting a backhand
topspin lob).

Students in athletic, artistic, and intellectual skill tutorials should
be given frequent opportunities to hone their skills. Coaches often guide
such practice sessions through a "stop action" format in which students
frequently are stopped and given suggestions for improvement before
continuing. By correcting mistakes as they occur, and by demonstrating
desirable techniques, coaches point the way to student improvement.

Coaches should be careful, however, that they do not destroy student motivation either by withholding praise or by stifling student creativity. In addition to correcting and demonstrating, coaches also can invite student reactions to their observations and can praise improved student performances. Mistakes are as easily corrected by queries and suggestions as they are by commands.

Serving as Supervisor

TAs also work with students individually as supervisors of internships in education, business, or government. The supervisory process consists of two related kinds of activities: gathering information and providing evaluative feedback.

Gathering Information   The supervisor's primary vehicle for gathering information is observation. While observing students in intern placements, TAs usually try to be unobtrusive. By so doing, they avoid interfering with the intern's relationship with student, customer, or client. They normally take detailed notes to help them reconstruct occurrences during a subsequent conversation with the student intern. In addition to observation, TA supervisors also gather information by talking privately with on-site supervisors of the intern and with other persons with whom the intern has contact. Since such conversations require tact and discretion, supervisory assistantships are often reserved for TAs who are mature and interpersonally competent.

Providing Evaluative Feedback   After gathering information, TA supervisors normally confer with student interns about their experiences. In conducting such conferences, supervisors may assume either a directive or nondirective style. Directive supervisors provide guidelines, directions, principles, and criticism. Directive supervisors have a model in mind of what's right and what's wrong and they don't mind informing interns how they measure up. This is how a directive teacher education supervisor might sound:

> *Supervisor:* I think you need to plan your activities better, be clearer about what you intend to do. You seemed to be unsure sometimes, and this is when the children got loud and unruly.
>
> *Teacher:* (Glancing at the pupils as they file in) That's a good point. I thought I had planned well, but the pupils had a difficult time understanding what to do.
>
> *Supervisor:* Good. Try to work on that. Also, for a review session you didn't seem to cover very much—just similes and metaphors and matching the main characters to the stories. The lesson moved too slowly. You need to cover more topics. This would help with the

discipline, too. (Bell rings) Well, I can see you need to get started. Do you think you can work on these ideas?

Teacher: Yes. Thanks for coming.

Supervisor: I enjoyed it. (Teacher rises and walks supervisor to the door.)[9]

As this example suggests, directive supervisors may be seen as brisk and straightforward. They may also be perceived, however, as self-righteous, judgmental, and lacking in empathy.

Nondirective supervisors, on the other hand, seek to act more on the tutorial model, attempting to guide student interns through a process of self-discovery. TAs using this approach ask interns why they chose a certain strategy, whether the strategy was effective, and what alternative strategies they might consider in similar future situations. When interns ask for advice, nondirective supervisors resist the impulse to provide answers. Instead, they lead interns to their own answers by using nondirective feedback techniques such as those that follow:[10]

1. *Refer to actions rather than actors.* Instead of saying, "You took a long time getting the interview started," a nondirective supervisor might note, "The preliminary portion of the interview took seven minutes. Why was that true?" Centering on the problematic behavior, as though it were independent of the person displaying it, can help to reduce the defensiveness of the student receiving feedback. This technique is consistent with the old adage, "Hate the sin but love the sinner."

2. *Offer observations rather than inferences.* Supervisors should focus their comments around actual occurrences rather than around a set of speculative conclusions, assertions, or psychological analyses arrived at by the supervisor. Thus, instead of inferring that an intern teacher was "ill-prepared for a class period," the supervisor might observe that "several student questions were not correctly answered." When this objective approach is used, the inferences to be drawn from an observation become the responsibility of the intern and the supervisor in consort rather than the supervisor alone.

3. *Provide descriptions rather than judgments.* Judgments include terms such as right, wrong, good, bad, effective, and ineffective. Descriptions, on the other hand, report events in neutral terms. For example, instead of labeling a legislative intern's behavior as "unsatisfactory," a nondirective supervisor would observe, "Senator Firm seemed to feel that you were late for your meeting with her today. She also seemed upset because you didn't have some report ready that she wanted. I also noticed

that she seemed impatient during your explanation. Did you think so, too?" While judgments are likely to make an intern defensive, descriptions help the supervisor and the intern to reach a common understanding of what occurred during an observed interaction.

4. *Suggest questions rather than answers.* An internship is designed to provide an opportunity for a student to act like a professional person in a field of endeavor. Since professional people are expected to exercise judgment in the face of problems, supervisors can be of greater value if they pose provocative questions than if they offer answers or advice. During conferences, interns should feel an identification with their supervisors and should feel confident that together they can generate useful ideas, guidelines, and plans. Instead of suggesting that an intern put in more hours, a nondirective supervisor might ask, "How many hours are you expected to work?"

Serving as Undergraduate Advisor

On occasion, teaching assistants are asked to be departmental advisors to undergraduate students. In this capacity, TAs must understand college requirements and departmental programs of study. Ideally, undergraduate advisors should also have knowledge of individual courses in the departmental curriculum.

In a typical advising session, the undergraduate advisor begins by asking questions to determine the student's status, interests, and needs. Given this information, the advisor offers an analysis of the advisee's situation regarding college and departmental requirements. In some cases it is necessary to discourage the student from pursuing a major because he or she does not meet departmental expectations. In other cases it is necessary to inform students about work that must be completed before admission to a departmental major. In still other cases it is appropriate to encourage students to pursue a program of study in the department because their needs and interests are compatible with departmental foci. Finally, for those students who are adequately prepared, the advisor helps them plan a suitable schedule for the remaining terms in their undergraduate careers.

While departmental advisors are expected to provide direction, they are not expected to free students from responsibility for their own undergraduate careers. Advisors cannot tell undergraduate students which courses or sections to take. Rather, advisors provide objective descriptions of alternatives from which undergraduates may choose.

Undergraduate advisors are also expected to have information about careers and graduate study opportunities in the subject-matter field. The undergraduate advisor's office should be well stocked with materials related to careers and with graduate school catalogues and other descriptive materials.

Being the undergraduate advisor of a department is a difficult task. A TA in this position must be well informed, caring, and personable. He or she must take the time to understand the needs and interests of students and must provide advice that is accurate and useful.

Directing Laboratory Sections

TAs facilitate student learning in a third context—laboratory sections. Laboratory sections are, by their very nature, characterized by peer interaction and active learning. While people often associate laboratory sections with the sciences, lab sections may be found in courses representing the social sciences and the humanities as well. Among the social science disciplines that sometimes offer laboratory sections are psychology and social work. Research methods courses across the social sciences often have laboratory sections. Similarly, humanities courses in areas such as art, dance, film, broadcasting, journalism, music, and theatre often include laboratory sections. When one adds to this list laboratory sections in the physical sciences (e.g., genetics, chemistry, geology, meteorology, physics, and zoology) and in courses in engineering, computer science, communication disorders, geography, and urban and regional planning, the pervasiveness of laboratory sections in a modern university becomes apparent.

While the role of a laboratory TA differs somewhat across disciplines, a number of general precepts apply to all such assignments. In this section, a chronology of advice for laboratory TAs will be provided. It should be noted, however, that since laboratory TAs also lecture, lead discussions, assess student progress, and provide other services, much of the content of previous and subsequent chapters pertains to laboratory TAs as well.

The Prepreparatory Phase

Since laboratory assignments often presume special TA knowledge or skill, it is important that TAs begin preparation as early as possible. Among the prepreparatory activities in which lab TAs may engage are the following.

Preview Textual Materials and Laboratory Manuals Because laboratory sections are often attached to lecture courses, TAs must become familiar with the textual materials used in the lecture as well as with manuals and other materials used in the laboratory section. When possible, TAs should discuss laboratory section expectations with the course director in advance of the first laboratory section meeting.

Become Familiar with Laboratory Equipment and Supplies   Well before the first meeting, lab TAs should familiarize themselves with the laboratory, studio, or other instructional space in which the laboratory section will take place. Since laboratory sections often involve equipment, TAs should experiment with all major equipment well in advance. They should also find out where necessary supplies are stored and ascertain who is responsible for ordering course materials. TAs should also be familiar with procedures for coping with equipment breakdown.

Learn about Safety Rules and Procedures   Some laboratory sections have the potential for student injury if procedures are not followed in a careful way. If safety rules for the laboratory have been established, the TA should publicize and enforce them. If safety rules have not been established, and if the potential for student injury exists, the individual TA is well advised to create such rules for his or her section. In addition, TAs should understand procedures for coping with emergencies. TAs who anticipate and develop procedures for coping with anything that can go wrong will not waste precious time at moments of crisis.

The Preparatory Phase   In preparing for a given laboratory period, a number of measures are appropriate. Good laboratory meetings depend as much on what the TA does before the meeting as during the meeting.

Perform the Learning Task   Since most laboratory meetings require that students do something, TAs can prepare for the lab by doing the thing they will ask their students to do. In the sciences, this normally means doing the experiments in the lab manuals. In the social sciences and humanities, TAs can complete the activity, create the product, or perform the act that will be required of their students. By so doing, TAs can ensure that the experiment or the learning activity works. As the UCLA handbook notes, "There is no guarantee it's going to work as advertised in the lab manual."[11]

Understand Theoretical and Historical Underpinnings   In preparing for a lab session, a TA should understand the larger theory to which an experiment or a learning activity is related. The UCLA manual provides a practical reason: "Otherwise, some students will hit you with a question you can't answer."[12] But more important, theoretical and historical background can make a laboratory period more interesting; for example, "Galileo did this whole thing using a cathedral lantern for a pendulum and the pulse for a watch!"[13] When students see the importance and relevance of what they are being asked to do, the experiment or activity takes on greater meaning.

Prepare Lab Notes and Materials   Although labs normally revolve around experiments or projects, TAs should plan for the meeting as carefully as they would plan for a discussion section or an autonomous course meeting. When preparing notes for later use in labs, TAs should think through and make notations about the entire laboratory period. Handouts should also be drafted during the preparatory phase.

The Introductory Phase

The first laboratory meeting is very important. It sets the tone for all subsequent meetings. Among the functions that might be served by the first meeting of a lab section are the following.

Getting Acquainted   TAs sometimes cancel the first scheduled lab meeting because students haven't been given enough material in lecture to warrant an experiment or project. This is a mistake. As chapter 3 noted, the first class period provides an excellent opportunity for students to get acquainted with each other and with the TA. Since laboratory groups tend to be small, the students should know each other by name and should develop a sense of group cohesion and rapport.

Clarifying Laboratory Section Expectations   The first period should acquaint students with lab section procedures and policies. When appropriate, an overview of laboratory or studio equipment may be presented. Students should receive a section plan or syllabus on which required materials and the focus of each lab meeting are noted. Related

Lab TAs often demonstrate the use of equipment such as this infrared thermography camera.

reading assignments should be indicated as well. Information about grading policy, attendance, makeup labs, and quizzes or examinations should also be provided in the first lab. Students should also be told about special expectations regarding the format of lab reports or projects. The University of California–Davis handbook urges TAs to specify such expectations in a detailed and specific manner.[14]

Providing Motivation   While laboratory sections exist for the purpose of promoting middle- to high-level cognitive learning, they also should provide an enjoyable social experience. By their very nature, lab sections invite students to work with and talk to each other. Labs and studios do not have to be deadly quiet places. Students should be talking, moving around, laughing, and getting the job done. Professionals working together in labs enjoy their interactions; students should do the same. One important function of the first day is to inform students that you will try to make the lab experience enjoyable; then proceed to meet your promise.

Conducting Laboratory Meetings

In ordinary lab meetings, TAs behave in highly predictable ways—which is as it should be. A typical lab period unfolds as follows.

Getting Started   TAs often begin a lab by taking attendance and providing a preview of the lab meeting. Some TAs briefly review the last lecture and check on student understanding of assigned readings.

Defining the Task   It is important that the experiments or projects to be completed during the lab be explained in a clear and precise way. Some TAs place the assignment on the chalkboard as well as announce it orally. On occasion, the nature of the task may be illustrated through demonstration or by examination of samples prepared by the TA or former students. In defining the task, the TA should also provide estimates of the time required for major lab activities.

Providing Needed Information and Materials   It is often necessary for TAs to explain procedures or to provide necessary background information. Such explanations should contain only information that is essential to performing the experiment or engaging in the activity. When necessary information has been provided, TAs should distribute materials that will be used during the lab meeting.

Supervising Student Work   As students work on assigned tasks in small groups, TAs are well advised to float and interact. When groups are experiencing difficulty, TAs should ask process questions: for example, How did you begin? Where did you first experience difficulty?

Are there other options available to you? TAs should resist the impulse to jump right in and complete the task for the students. TAs should also refrain from interrupting students by making frequent whole-class observations about how things are going or by providing information that should have been given at the beginning of the lab period.

Ensuring Summary and Synthesis   At the end of the lab period, students should be asked to put away materials and come together as a large group. This is an appropriate time to debrief students about their experiences and to be certain that students have drawn appropriate conclusions from their work. TAs normally provide summary and synthesis through leading a class discussion rather than by lecturing.

Adding New Wrinkles   After conducting a laboratory meeting, some TAs find it helpful to evaluate what happened and to write suggestions for modifying the experiment or project for future use. There is nothing sacred about experiments in a lab manual or learning activities in a lab file. As TAs acquire experience, they can improve materials used in lab sections by refining them or by thinking of creative extensions to them.

Summary

TAs are often expected to facilitate student learning or growth. When this is their primary mission, they are not expected to simply lecture, lead class discussions, or otherwise keep students in whole-class structures. Rather, they are expected to work individually and in small groups with students as they guide, help, and encourage them to acquire knowledge, skill, and a sense of direction.

When teaching autonomous sections of skill courses, TAs may elect either the student-centered or the process-centered approach to instruction. When following the student-centered approach, TAs often give students project options and encourage them to set personal goals, timetables, and instructional regimens. When electing a process-centered approach, TAs plan a careful sequence of instruction sometimes involving precepts, examples, performances, and evaluations.

TAs also facilitate student learning by working with students individually. Among the one-on-one relationships TAs establish with students are serving as tutor, as writing lab instructor, as coach, as supervisor, and as undergraduate advisor. In each of these situations TAs establish close personal relationships with individual students.

Finally, TAs facilitate student learning by directing their work in laboratory sections. Laboratory TAs must engage in a good deal of preparation, including becoming familiar with laboratory equipment, learning about safety rules and procedures, practicing experiments or other learning tasks, and reading relevant textual, theoretical, and historical materials. Since laboratory TAs are expected to facilitate the work of their students, they must get acquainted with them, clarify lab section expectations, provide motivation, and conduct effective laboratory sections. As with all TAs assigned to facilitative contexts, laboratory TAs are expected to take a personal interest in the progress of their students.

Notes

1. Barbara Schneider Fuhrmann and Anthony F. Grasha, *A Practical Handbook for College Teachers* (Boston: Little, Brown and Company, 1983), p. 294. Used with permission.
2. Syllabus, "Swimming I," Department of Physical Education and Dance, University of Wisconsin–Madison, no date, p. 1.
3. "Swimming I," p. 1.
4. Howard L. Stone, "Guiding Students to Discover," Educational Resources, Center for Health Sciences, University of Wisconsin–Madison, no date, p. 1.
5. Stone, p. 2.
6. Stone, p. 2.
7. Stone, p. 2.
8. Deborah Kransler, "The Role of the Graduate Teaching Assistant" (videotape), Center for Instructional Development and Research, University of Washington, May 1985.
9. Charles A. Reavis, *Teacher Improvement Through Clinical Supervision* (Bloomington, Ind.: Phi Delta Kappa Educational Foundation, 1978), pp. 5–6.
10. These four techniques were inspired by a longer list entitled "Aids for Giving and Receiving Feedback," unpublished manuscript, Department of Psychology, University of California, Los Angeles, no date, pp. 1–3.
11. *The TA at UCLA: 1984–85 Handbook* (Los Angeles: University of California at Los Angeles, 1984), p. 34.
12. *The TA at UCLA,* p. 34.
13. *The TA at UCLA,* p. 34.
14. *TA Handbook* (Davis: Teaching Resources Center, University of California–Davis, no date), p. 26.

9

Assessing Student Learning

"As a teacher-scholar-human being, you are well aware that your skills in classroom testing have important, direct effects on the lives of those whom you examine. Our society is structured in such a way that testing is one of the most important activities in which you engage at the University. The ethical implications of your role in testing are at least as important as your academic expectancies and standards."[1]

Robert M. Murphey
"Classroom Test Construction"

Tests profoundly affect the lives of college students. Undergraduates spend a great deal of time preparing for, worrying about, and taking examinations. The stress created by tests has earned a name for itself in the annals of psychological maladies: test anxiety. Given the importance assigned to tests by students, universities, and employers, TAs may not take testing lightly. College instructors are ethically bound to assess student work in a careful, fair, and comprehensive manner.

Given the vital role of testing, it is important, nonetheless, to recognize that testing is but one component in the assessment process; therefore, this chapter begins by considering the broad nature of assessment and alternatives to testing before turning to matters of test construction and utilization. The concluding sections consider the evaluation and grading process.

The Nature of Assessment

Assessment is an inclusive term used to refer to the process of gathering and judging data about students. It consists of a number of possible components, serves a variety of purposes, and occurs at various stages in the learning process.

The Components of Assessment

Assessment consists of two essential ingredients: measurement and evaluation.[2] Measurement refers to anything the TA may do to try to determine the status of student cognitive, affective, or psychomotor behaviors. While the terms tests and measurement are sometimes equated, tests are but one form of measurement. A number of other forms exist including some that have nothing to do with the grade a student will receive.

As tests are to measurement, grades are to evaluation. Many students equate grades and evaluation because grades are the only evaluation they receive. Since some instructors do not return final examinations, hoping to preserve their confidentiality for future generations of students, a student may receive no more of an evaluation than a grade posted impersonally on an office door. While grades are definitely one form of evaluation, they are not the only form available. Evaluation should occur on a daily basis, not just when it's time to record an alphabetic letter in the grade book.

The Purposes of Assessment

TAs may engage in assessment for a number of reasons. One important reason is to provide information regarding the results of instruction. TAs may also assess in order to find out what students already know, to discover student likes and dislikes, to make decisions about future course changes, to provide feedback for the course director, or to secure personal feedback. Even if it were not necessary to submit grades to the registrar, TAs would still wish to engage in assessment, both measurement and evaluation. The essence of good teaching is inviting and being sensitive to student feedback, evaluating such feedback, and responding appropriately in the light of such feedback.

Assessment can take place at any time. When categorized according to time, the three forms of assessment are preassessment, formative assessment, and summative assessment.

The Timing of Assessment

Preassessment   Preassessment takes place before instruction begins. Preassessment may be used to place students into appropriate courses, or to exempt students who already have the knowledge or skills in question, or to discover which areas of knowledge should receive the most attention.

Formative Assessment   Formative assessment takes place during the instructional process. It enables TAs to discover how well the students have understood the information or mastered given tasks. It also helps TAs to identify areas that require additional instruction and to modify strategies that aren't working. Formative assessment is vital to effective teaching. If you don't know how you are doing, you will have no basis for change or growth.

Summative Assessment   Summative assessment occurs at the conclusion of a unit of study. It enables TAs to judge the success of instruction, to modify plans for subsequent units of study (where appropriate), and, of course, to provide a grade for the student.

Since the purpose of assessment is to discover the status of student behavior and to make judgments about the quality of that behavior, it should be apparent that a test may not be the only or the best way of getting data. In this section, some alternative means of assessment are explored.[3]

Test-free Assessment

One of the easiest ways to find out how students are doing is to gather work samples. This is a popular strategy in laboratory sections. TAs simply gather and inspect lab reports to ensure that experiments or projects are being conducted properly. While lab TAs in the sciences tend to record grades for each lab assignment, one need not necessarily do so. For example, TAs in television labs often gather bits and pieces of a project (e.g., idea form, storyboard, script) just to ensure that students are making progress; the graded evaluation awaits completion of the televised program.

Work Samples

Discussion section TAs, who use small-group alternatives to whole class discussions, will also wish to examine work samples. This may be done by gathering and evaluating handouts or work sheets or by having participants from the small groups share their progress in a whole-class discussion. In both lab sections and discussion sections, TAs often move around the room observing small groups at work and providing spontaneous reactions when appropriate.

Self-reports

If you wish to discover things about people, one of the most direct means is to ask them. Some kinds of information are available only through self-reports. For example, if you wish to find out something about your students' attitudes or interests you will, of necessity, have to trust them to tell you the truth. You might hand out a list of propositions or a list of leisure-time activities and have them rank each item on the list from one (strongly agree/do it all the time) to seven (strongly disagree/never do it).

Some TAs gather self-reports from students during the first class meeting. The information gleaned through such reports can be used to adjust course content to student interests and needs. Fuhrmann and Grasha go a step beyond by recommending that students be invited to "specify content areas, teaching methods, and projects" they would like included in the course and "indicate . . . contributions they might make to the course given their backgrounds and experiences."[4] When used in this way, self-reports can increase student input into course decision making.

Peer Reports

Peers can enrich the assessment process by providing additional points of view regarding each others' work. In addition to providing a personal evaluation of student oral and written work, TAs may require peers to provide similar evaluations. While peer evaluations do not normally influence grades awarded by TAs, students may use them as evidence to support an allegation of TA assessment inaccuracy. For example, a TA using an analytic scale such as the one provided in table 9.1 may question his or her own conclusion that the main points were vague if peers were able to identify the main points with precision in the appropriate comments section of the analytic scale. For analytic scales to be of real value, they should call for explicit student judgments.

On some occasions, peer reports may be a primary vehicle for student assessments. For example, in a group discussion course in which students are required to complete a group task outside of class, the evaluation of students by their peers may be the best possible evidence about students who did their fair share and students who did not. When peer reports are to be permitted to influence TA assessment, students should

Table 9.1. Analytic Scale for Student Oral Reports.

Speaker _____ Date _____

Topic _____ Rater _____

	Strong				Weak	Comments
Introduction	5	4	3	2	1	
Creates interest						
Announces topic						
Previews content						
Organization of body	5	4	3	2	1	
Clear main points						
Strong transitions						
Conclusion	5	4	3	2	1	
Summarizes content						
Effects closure						
Content of report	5	4	3	2	1	
Carefully documented						
Relevant						
Delivery	5	4	3	2	1	
Effective vocal behavior						
Effective physical behavior						
Language	5	4	3	2	1	
Correct						
Clear						
Vivid						

be apprised of this fact early in the term. Furthermore, procedures for detecting peer collusion should be invented and validated. One system for encouraging honest peer evaluations is to require students to rank-order the contributions of all members of their group other than themselves.

Written Projects

A wide variety of written projects may provide evidence of student learning. TAs in discussion sections or autonomous sections may assign questions in the text that students are to complete as homework. Research suggests that writing can enhance the learning process. Some universities are recommending that students be encouraged to write across the curriculum.

TAs who wish to establish an ongoing discussion with students about the course may use *dialogue journals*.[5] Such journals provide an opportunity for students to reflect on what they are learning. TAs gather the journals periodically and respond in writing to the thoughts of each student. Dialogue journals are an effective means of establishing a personal relationship with students. Such journals may be used as a substitute for more traditional kinds of writing assignments.

When a term paper or other major writing assignment is made, TAs should identify the goals of the project. TAs may also provide a time line including bench-mark dates when various aspects of the project are to be completed. TAs who simply assign a term paper at the beginning of the semester and scrawl comments on the completed paper at the end of the semester have not provided a rich learning experience. As the student's independent work unfolds, the TA should provide encouragement, feedback, advice, necessary instruction, and eventually, final evaluation.

Oral Projects

In some courses, the most important form of assessment is oral in nature. For example, in foreign language and public speaking courses the student's ability to use language in social contexts is often assigned the highest priority. In other courses, TAs assign oral projects rather than written ones so that all students profit from each others' work.

When assigning oral projects that will be assessed, TAs should be especially careful about clarifying their expectations. Sometimes it is helpful for the TA to provide an example through demonstration or videotape. If an analytic scale (see Table 9.1) is to be used during the assessment, a copy of the scale should be distributed at the time the assignment is made. TAs should talk their way through the scale, clarifying each feature about which a judgment will be rendered.

This section begins by considering three principles for constructing tests. It then considers how essay tests are constructed and graded and how objective test questions are written and assembled.

Two of the most important concepts related to test development are embraced by the labels validity and reliability. Beyond these two traditional concepts there is still another concept that helps to guide test development: appropriateness to instructional goals.

Ensure That the Test Has Content Validity   Content validity is the most important concept related to test development. Quite simply, content validity refers to how well a test samples from the broad range of information or skills that a unit or course seeks to impart or develop. Whatever the range of content or skill covered by a test—a week, six weeks, a quarter, or a semester—a test with content validity includes items related to each major content or skill area covered during the test period. When students walk away from an examination feeling that they studied the right material, the examination probably has content validity. When students walk away from an exam grumbling, "It didn't cover a third of the stuff I studied," the examination is probably grossly lacking in content validity.

Strive for Test Reliability   When engaging in measurement, TAs hope that the scores they derive are reliable indicators of student performance. In general, a measurement is reliable if intelligent students who have prepared carefully earn higher scores than less intelligent students who have coasted.

In objective tests, low reliability is caused by poorly constructed items that do not differentiate between students who possess the knowledge and students who do not. Test length is also related to reliability. Longer objective tests are a more reliable indicator of student knowledge than shorter tests. On a ten-item true–false test, for example, students have a strong probability of guessing five correctly even without studying; however, on a fifty-item test knowledgeable students are likely to rise to the top.

Reliability also refers to the consistency of the rater's judgments. For example, TAs who grade essay examination responses often wonder if they would assign the same numerical score were they to reread the essays tomorrow, the day after, or the day after that. Such nagging self-doubts are related to the issue of reliability. To check on their consistency, TAs can grade several exams or essays first, recording the scores on a separate sheet of paper. They may then shuffle the exams or essays back into the pile to be graded. When all papers are graded, TAs can compare the consistency of the two sets of scores for the sample papers.

If more than one TA is to grade a set of exams, it may be possible to increase consistency by having the same TA grade certain questions across all the exams. When grading papers that may not be divided into chunks, multiple TAs can strive for consistency by devising mutually acceptable criteria and by comparing grades for several papers using those criteria.

Match Test Strategies to Instructional Goals   As was noted in chapter 4, once instructors have identified instructional goals they are well on the way to identifying necessary instructional strategies and necessary means of instructional assessment. Some even have suggested that test questions ought to be written at the time instructional objectives for a course are determined.[6] By so doing, TAs will acquire a very clear understanding of their final expectations.

But more important than the issue of when one writes questions is the matter of the appropriateness of the questions one writes. Certain test forms and types of questions are more suitable for some cognitive levels than for others. True–false and completion questions are most often used for testing student recall and comprehension but not higher-order thinking skills. Matching questions can be used to test recall-, comprehension-, and application-level behaviors and multiple-choice questions are used to test these three levels plus analysis, if the test provides something to be analyzed. The most frequently used format for testing student analysis, synthesis, and evaluation behaviors is the essay test. Test questions and formats should reflect course objectives and strategies. TAs who merely teach at the recall and comprehension levels have given up any legitimate right to test at the analysis or synthesis levels. Similarly, TAs who have spent the semester trying to improve the critical thinking skills of their students will not test instructional success by giving a 100-item true–false final examination.

Constructing and Grading Essay Tests

The greatest single advantage of essay tests is that they permit TAs to test at the higher cognitive levels. Students are required to formulate, organize, and amplify a response. The greatest disadvantage of essay tests is that they are difficult to score, leading to reader subjectivity that may seriously jeopardize test reliability. Since this is true, essay tests should be constructed and graded in a careful manner.

Guidelines for Writing Essay Tests   When course objectives demand an essay test, it should be carefully developed. Four guidelines pertain:

1. *Use a variety of essay items.*[7] An essay test with a single question is not likely to have content validity. Even if it did, it would function at such a high level of abstraction that it would be very

difficult to grade. By increasing the number of items and reducing the response time and the breadth of questions, TAs can test a greater variety of course objectives and can do so with considerably less subjectivity.

2. *Focus questions precisely.* Essay items should call for a relatively precise student response. Essay questions that are general and vague are hard to answer and grade. The questions should be so written that they "define the parameters of expected answers as clearly as possible."[8]

3. *Test your questions by answering them.* For each essay item, TAs are well advised to provide a model answer for the question and to determine the number of points that should be awarded to each of the essential components of the response. TAs who wait until after the exam to decide on grading criteria may discover that they really didn't have a clear response in mind or, if they did, that it is long forgotten.

4. *Limit question alternatives.* Some instructors offer choices of questions on essay tests. For example, students are instructed to choose two questions from part A, two from part B, and two from part C. Assuming that in this case each part has four questions, each student is selecting six out of twelve questions. By offering alternatives of this sort, instructors make it possible for students to avoid half of the test material—the half that each student considers most difficult. Students with knowledge sufficient to answer only six questions could earn an A just as easily as students capable of competently answering all twelve. If students are to be compared, shouldn't they take the same test?

Guidelines for Grading Essay Tests   Recognizing that essay tests are especially susceptible to grader subjectivity, TAs should strive to grade tests as objectively as possible. The reliability of an essay test will be enhanced by the consistent application of objective standards. The following guidelines will help to promote reliable grading of essay tests.

1. *Grade tests anonymously.* To avoid being influenced by previous student work, TAs may choose to grade tests in an anonymous fashion. Students can be asked to put their names on the inside rear cover of their bluebooks or exam forms rather than on the front page.

2. *Grade all responses to a single essay item at one time.* Rather than grading each exam booklet totally before moving on to the next booklet, TAs can enhance the reliability of their judgments by grading one essay question or item at a time. By so doing, TAs need keep only one answer key in mind at a time.

Grading papers and examinations can be an intellectually demanding and time-consuming task for TAs.

3. *Be certain to judge content rather than literary style.* It is difficult to overlook errant syntax, misspellings, improper punctuation, and other flaws in composition. Still, when grading essay examinations TAs should focus primary attention on the accuracy and completeness of student responses to questions. In English composition courses, however, writing competence may be a major or primary factor in grading essay examinations.

4. *When returning essay examinations, include a model answer to each item.* Student motivation is at a high point when essay examination grades are received. To capitalize on this motivation, TAs can distribute sample essay item responses so that students can find out how their responses differed from a desired response.

Constructing Objective Tests

Objective tests have a number of advantages: they can be varied and interesting, they can survey a wide variety of material, they are time efficient during the examination period, they may be easily and quickly scored, and, when properly constructed, they have both content validity and reliability. Objective tests do, however, have limitations: objective tests take time to construct, do not lend themselves easily to assessment of higher-order cognitive behaviors, and are subject to student guessing and misinterpretations. In this section, the four standard kinds of objective test items will be considered. Some general guidelines for putting the objective test together will then be considered.

Writing True–False Items   True–false items demand that a student judge a statement to be correct or incorrect. In terms of form, a true–false statement identifies a concept and an attribute associated with the concept. While the concept is an accurate statement, the attribute associated with the concept may be either true or false. For example, consider the following true–false item: "The phrase 'ontogeny recapitulates phylogeny' means that the development of the individual parallels the development of human kind." The first part of this question is factually accurate since the phrase "ontogeny recapitulates phylogeny" is a well-known concept. The student must determine if the phrase following the words "means that" is a correct or incorrect attribute of that concept. In this case the answer is true.

Over the years, a general consensus concerning the proper format of true–false test items and true–false test structures has emerged. Among the truisms of true–false testing are the following:[9]

1. The words all, never, no, and always should be avoided since they suggest that the correct answer is "false."

2. The words usually, sometimes, and maybe should be avoided since they suggest that the correct answer is "true."

3. Exact wording from the textbook or a lecture should be avoided since such items are picky.

4. Trivial reasons for a statement being correct or incorrect should be avoided because such items are tricky.

5. A statement should not contain both true attributes and untrue attributes. Such items are also tricky.

6. Double negatives, figurative language, and ambiguous language in a question should be avoided since they test reading ability rather than knowledge of the subject matter.

7. True–false questions should be arranged in a random fashion. Patterned arrangements of true and false statements may mislead students.

8. True–false items should be clustered in such a way that adjacent questions concern comparable subject matter.

9. True–false examinations may be modified to enable students to provide a rationale for their answers when they feel a question is ambiguous. When using a modified examination, TAs may score a true–false item as either correct or incorrect in the light of the rationale for the answer provided by the students.

Writing and Grading Completion Items   Completion items require students to supply a word or words that have been omitted from a statement. These items efficiently test lower-order cognitive behaviors and they are easy to write. Completion items are, however, often dull and reflect a "guess what I'm thinking" test mentality. Among the truisms for completion item construction are the following:[10]

1. Exact textbook language should be avoided.
2. The desired response should be brief.
3. The desired response should be exact. Ambiguous completion items enable multiple correct responses.
4. The desired response should be a significant concept rather than a minute detail.
5. When students are being asked to recall a number of points, it is easier to provide a direction or question with space for the answer than it is to imbed blanks within the statement.
6. Statement form should not provide cues to the answer; for example, blanks should be of the same length and the designations "a(n)" and "(s)" should be used when appropriate.
7. Completion items need not invite simple mindless recall; completion questions can function at the comprehension and even the application levels of cognition; for example, "Chlorophyta are to the _____ period as _____ are to the Silurian period."
8. The key for the completion section of an examination should identify all acceptable answers for each blank.

Writing Matching Items   Matching questions can be a good deal of fun both for the exam writer and for the exam takers. Matching questions consist of directions and two columns of material. The student is instructed to match the material in column B with the material in column A. One of the advantages of matching questions is that they can cover a great deal of material in a highly efficient manner. Matching questions are also very popular with students, who find them more interesting than other objective item formats. One of the disadvantages of matching items is that they tend to be less difficult than the other forms (maybe that's why students are so fond of them). The following generalizations pertain to matching items:[11]

1. The items in columns A and B should all be related in the same way. For example, column A may consist of terms and column B may consist of definitions, or column A may consist of events and column B may consist of dates.

2. The stem of the matching item should clearly identify the relationship of the two columns; for example, "Match the patterns of organization in column A with their descriptions in column B."

3. Distractor items may be included in column B to make the task more difficult. When this is done, the existence of distractors should be explained in the stem; for example, "Caution: three of the entries in column B do not apply."

4. Answer blanks are normally placed to the left of each entry in column A.

5. Column B is normally placed at the right-hand side of the page.

6. The number of entries in columns A and B should not exceed ten to fifteen entries per matching item.

7. Whenever possible, all entries in columns A and B should be placed on the same page.

Writing Multiple-choice Items   The multiple-choice question is the most popular item format for standardized tests. It is also a popular choice for exams composed by TAs. Multiple-choice questions may be written at most cognitive levels. Through a program of testing and revision, multiple-choice tests can be made into highly reliable instruments. Multiple-choice questions are, however, more difficult to write than other item formats. The following caveats pertain to multiple-choice items:[12]

1. The stem in a multiple-choice item should be unambiguous and complete. It should contain all information necessary for an informed choice and it should be expressed in clear language.

2. The stem should ask students to identify the best answer when a response option other than the correct answer is partially correct.

3. The response options should be so written that one answer is clearly correct under careful and knowledgeable scrutiny.

4. The response options should be so written that incorrect answers will appear plausible to uninformed students.

5. The response options should be roughly parallel in structure, in length, in content, and in the use of technical language.

6. It is generally wise to avoid "all of the above" as the final response option since students able to identify a single incorrect answer also know that "all of the above" is an incorrect response.

7. Correct responses should be assigned response positions in such a manner that they appear equally at positions ABCDE.

Assembling the Objective Test   In addition to constructing individual items, TAs often are required to put together a complete examination. The following guidelines are helpful:[13]

1. Each item in an objective test should test different content. By following this guideline, TAs can ensure content validity by sampling widely from unit or course content.
2. Each item in an objective test should stand alone. It should neither cue the answer to another question nor be dependent on answers to previous questions.
3. The items in the examination should not be arranged in the same order in which they were presented in the course or textbook. Such an order might provide answer cues.
4. All items written in the same item format should be clustered together in the test.
5. Be certain that the test can be completed in the available examination time. It is sometimes recommended that exams be so written that 95 percent of the students are able to complete the test in the allotted time.

To Compare or Not to Compare

There are two major approaches to assessment: norm-referenced assessment and criterion-referenced assessment. Each approach requires special assessment skills. Norm-referenced assessment demands that TAs learn to construct a grading scale while criterion-referenced assessment forces TAs to establish criteria for judging student work.

Constructing a Grading Scale

Most TAs grade on a curve. This means that the grades of individual students are influenced by the performances of their peers. In establishing a curve, TAs normally list the possible numerical scores that may be earned. The number of students receiving each score is then recorded. Having recorded the scores, TAs must then determine the cutoff point for each grade.

There are various means of determining cut-off points. One method is to pre-establish the percentage of specific grades to be awarded. For example, a TA may choose to give 10 percent As and Fs, 20 percent Bs and Ds, and 40 percent Cs. While this method rarely works perfectly, due to the clustering of scores, it does ensure that grades will be differentiated. It should be noted, however, that assigning percentages to specific grades is also arbitrary in that students with adjacent arithmetic scores may be awarded different letter grades.

A second method is to look for clusters of student scores with spaces or gaps between them on the list. The wider the gap between clusters of scores, the easier the TA's task and the more comfortable the TA feels about the decision. This procedure is, however, at the mercy of the particular grade distribution, and gaps may not point the way to grades being assigned across the spectrum.

Since both of the previous methods have merit, TAs often use a blend of the two in achieving what they consider a fair grade distribution. The TA may have in mind a cutoff point of 93 for an A but may accept 92 if a large number of students have such a score.

Another possible system is to establish a curve based upon the highest obtained score, and percentages thereof. For example, 90 to 100 percent of the highest score may be awarded an A, 80 to 89 percent a B, 70 to 79 percent a C, 60 to 69 percent a D, and less than 60 percent an F. This system is both objective and flexible, providing a clear procedure to be applied to each unique distribution of scores.

Finally, some TAs invent exotic grading systems in which points are assigned to each graded project during the course of the term. At the end of the term, the total points of students are summed and scaled. While there is nothing essentially wrong with such a point system, TAs may also wish to scale and record grades for the components along the way. This system enables students to know where they stand at each point in the course. Should the final curve give the student a lower grade than he or she would have received had the individual grades been weighted, summed, and converted to a letter grade, the higher of the two grades should be awarded.

In criterion-referenced assessment, TAs determine in advance what a student must do to receive each of the letter grades on a test, paper, or other course assignment. This does not always work to the student's advantage. For example, TAs may decide that on a 100-item test a score of 90 or better will be assigned an A, 80 to 89 a B, 70 to 79 a C, 60 to 69 a D, and 59 and below an F. Should the exam prove difficult for students, it is conceivable that no one would receive an A or even a B. On the other hand, if all students scored in the 80s or 90s, no one would receive a C, D, or F. While criterion-referenced scoring ensures that students who do well on tests will be suitably rewarded, most students, without really understanding the difference, probably prefer grading on the curve to grading against predetermined criteria.

When used for grading oral and written reports and essay exams, criterion-referenced assessment begins to look more qualitative than quantitative. TAs describe the features or criteria that must be present for each of the assigned grades to be awarded. When such criteria are distributed at the time an assignment is made, students can choose the grade they wish to strive for and can direct their energies accordingly.

Establishing Criteria for Judging Student Work

Computing Final Grades

Final grades often must be submitted a relatively short time after the final examination is given. Although end-of-term activities are demanding, TAs should strive for accuracy in computing their final grades.

Determining the Weight of Individual Assignments

TAs must decide (if it is not decided for them) how much weight to assign to each graded element of the courses or sections they teach. For example, a lab TA must assign weight to student scores on laboratory workbook experiments in comparison with student scores on lab quizzes. Similarly, lecturers in charge of independent courses must determine the weight to be assigned to tests, papers, homework assignments, and class participation. Ideally, students should be informed of the weight of each component at the beginning of the term.

Avoiding Arbitrariness in Grading

As TAs are looking ahead to final grade determinations, they should avoid the temptation to do silly things in the name of being "nice" to students. For example, TAs should not (1) assign different weights to assignments than those announced by the course director, (2) permit students to determine the weights to be assigned to their own work, (3) drop the lowest grade of each student, (4) eliminate the final examination for students who have earned As on earlier examinations, (5) permit students to write an extra-credit paper, or (6) substitute a paper for an examination. If instruction is to be fairly evaluated, all students should be expected to complete the same work.

Determining Final Grades

Once the weight of each grade has been determined and arbitrariness avoided, TAs need only choose and employ a system for computing final grades. The system for computing grades should be mathematically precise. It involves converting letter grades to number grades, multiplying each number grade by the percentage assigned to it, and totaling all products subsequently. After determining final numerical grades, TAs need only convert such grades to letter grades. Increasingly, instructors are using computorized spread sheets to record and determine grades.

Holding Grade Conferences

It is something of an understatement to note that students do not always agree with the grades they receive. At one time or another all TAs must deal with students who are upset or angry about a grade.

Preparing for Grade Conferences

When a student is upset about a grade, it is generally wise to avoid an impassioned discussion in the classroom setting. Rather, TAs should establish a time and place when a grading conference may be held. It is often wise to provide a "cooling-off period" prior to the grade conference.

It is important that TAs arrive at grade conferences well prepared for the interaction that will occur. Dianna Harbin, a TA at the University of Washington, recommends that TAs have all relevant paperwork present—the examination or paper, an answer key or criteria sheet, examples of excellent answers or papers. She also recommends that TAs understand the relationship of the work being complained about to course goals.[14]

During grade conferences, TAs must be responsive to student concerns while still maintaining academic standards. In order to do this, Harbin recommends that TAs identify the grading criteria that were employed, provide examples of a correct answer or an excellent paper, allow themselves time to decide about student requests, and inform students that the reasons for affirming or denying the request will be explained to them in writing.[15] Throughout the grading conference TAs should remain calm, friendly, and open-minded. If students have valid points, TAs should give them honest consideration. TAs must resist pressure to raise a grade simply because the student needs a higher grade to get into business school, graduate with honors, or stay off probation.

During the Grade Conference

After the grade conference, TAs should do as they promised in a relatively prompt manner. After reconsidering a response or paper, or talking with the professor about it, TAs should state their final decision and the reasons for that decision and mail that response to the concerned student. In the event the student's request is denied, the TA may wish to indicate avenues of appeal available to the student.

Following the Grade Conference

Assessment is an inclusive term used to refer to the process of gathering and judging data about students. It consists of measurement, one form of which is testing, and evaluation, one form of which is grading. Assessment serves a variety of purposes and may occur before, during, and after instruction. Forms of assessment other than testing include work samples, self-reports, peer reports, written projects, and oral projects. Certain principles of test development are useful when constructing tests: ensure that the test has content validity, strive for test reliability, and match test strategies to instructional goals. When constructing and grading essay tests, TAs should be especially careful since they are difficult to score and are prone to reader subjectivity. When constructing objective tests, TAs may follow guidelines for writing true–false, completion, matching, and multiple-choice items. Additional guidelines may be used when assembling objective tests. The issue of whether or not to compare students is an important one. TAs who believe in norm-referenced assessment will have occasion to construct a scale or curve.

Summary

Similarly, TAs who believe in criterion-referenced assessment must develop skill in establishing criteria for judging student work. In order to compute final grades, TAs must know or determine the weight of individual assignments, must avoid arbitrariness, and must determine final grades. Finally, through grade conferences, TAs must deal with students who are upset or angry about a grade.

Notes

1. Robert M. Murphey, "Classroom Test Construction," in *TA Handbook* (Davis: Teaching Resources Center, University of California, Davis, no date) p. 34.
2. The basic notion of assessment reflected in this section was taken from R. R. Allen, Kenneth L. Brown, and Joanne Yatvin, *Learning Language Through Communication: A Functional Perspective* (Belmont, Calif.: Wadsworth Publishing, 1986), pp. 395–98.
3. Some of the means of assessment identified in this section are also reported in Allen, Brown, and Yatvin, pp. 408–20.
4. Barbara Schneider Fuhrmann and Anthony F. Grasha, *A Practical Handbook for College Teachers* (Boston: Little, Brown and Company, 1983), p. 148.
5. Jana Staton, Joy Kreeft, and Shelley Gutstein, eds., *Dialogue: The Newsletter about Dialogue Journals* 2 (August 1983): entire issue.
6. Allen, Brown, and Yatvin, p. 407.
7. The guidelines presented in this section are based on those of K. D. Hopkins and J. C. Stanley, *Educational and Psychological Measurement and Evaluation* (Englewood Cliffs, N.J.: Prentice Hall, 1981), pp. 221–22.
8. *TAs As Teachers: A Handbook for Teaching Assistants at UCSB* (Santa Barbara: University of California at Santa Barbara, 1984), p. 29.
9. The guidelines in this section were influenced by *TAs As Teachers,* pp. 26–27 and Hopkins and Stanley, pp. 251–53.
10. The guidelines in this section were influenced by Hopkins and Stanley, pp. 261–63.
11. The guidelines in this section were influenced in part by Hopkins and Stanley, pp. 257–58.
12. The guidelines in this section were influenced in part by Hopkins and Stanley, pp. 242–48.
13. The guidelines in this section were influenced in part by Hopkins and Stanley, pp. 242–48.
14. Dianna Harbin, "The Role of the Graduate Teaching Assistant" (videotape) Center for Instructional Development and Research, University of Washington, May 1985.
15. Harbin.

10

Growing in Teaching Skill

"Given that teaching is a learning process, that it relies on corrective input from students, it follows that teaching is indeed a learnable skill, not an innate gift. Experience is a major factor in improvement, but active inquiry into one's own practice and effective use of available resources can accelerate experience significantly."[1]

Teaching Fellows Handbook
Harvard University

As this quotation observes, "teaching is indeed a learnable skill." Not all TAs, however, begin at the same starting point. Some TAs receive extraordinarily high student evaluations from their very first semester on campus, even when teaching courses outside their areas of primary expertise; such TAs, whatever they teach, are considered knowledgeable, well organized, and effective. Other TAs struggle a good deal as they strive to become effective teachers, even in courses in which they have considerable subject-matter expertise.

One may well ask, then, if some TAs are not more innately gifted than others. The honest answer is yes. TAs who are outgoing, articulate, well organized, friendly, compassionate, and witty may well begin a step or two up the ladder of TA effectiveness than their peers who lack these qualities. Still, TAs who experience initial difficulties need not look for a career outside of college teaching. TAs do grow through experience. But even more important, TAs grow through feedback from students, through the evaluations of supervisors and peers, through the careful monitoring of their own teaching, and through charting a personal course of self-improvement.

Securing Student Feedback

Not all feedback from students needs to be invited. Students provide both positive and negative feedback on a daily basis whether or not TAs ask for it. TAs need only be sensitive to student reactions. Libby Wood, in the University of California–Berkeley handbook, informs TAs that negative feedback may be inferred from a number of student actions: "Everyone reads during section, no one offers suggestions, attendance is down to your brother's best friend, and your section grades are worse than those of the other TAs."[2]

Unfortunately, TAs are not always adept at "reading" student feedback. Negative end-of-term teaching evaluations by students often come as a shock to TAs who are insensitive to the daily signs of student discontent. To avoid such trauma, TAs may wish to take the initiative by inviting student feedback earlier in the term when corrective action may still be taken. This section will consider both what to ask and how to ask it.

What to Ask Students about Your Teaching

End-of-term evaluation forms are often used by departments to secure student evaluations of teaching assistants. The items included on such instruments usually survey across a variety of areas of teaching competence, including the five that follow.

Questions about TA General Effectiveness   Questions about general effectiveness provide a synopsis of how well a TA is doing. The following questions are illustrative:

> Is the TA generally effective in carrying out assigned duties?
> Has the TA expanded your understanding of the subject?
> Has the TA challenged you intellectually?
> Is the TA knowledgeable about and interested in the subject matter?[3]

While such questions about general effectiveness need not involve comparisons with other TAs, some TAs wish such information. When this is true, a question such as "Does the TA compare favorably with other TAs you have known?" may be used.

Questions about TA Planning and Organization   Students expect their TAs to be well prepared for instruction. When their expectations are not met, end-of-term evaluations may reflect student dissatisfaction. Questions that help TAs to determine student perceptions of their preparedness and organization follow:

> Does the TA have a clear sense of the structure of the course or section?
> Does the TA clearly communicate course and section goals and expectations to students?
> Is the TA carefully prepared for each meeting?
> Is the TA conversant with textual materials and other assigned materials?
> Does the TA plan for and effectively use supplementary materials such as handouts, transparencies, and laboratory devices?[4]

Given a chance, most TAs would prefer to be thought of as being carefully prepared, well organized, and generally on top of things.

Questions about TA Classroom Communication   Having planned carefully, TAs must then be able to execute their plans through effective classroom communication. Among the range of questions TAs may ask about their classroom communication skills are the following:

> Does the TA communicate clearly and effectively through vocal and physical delivery?
> Does the TA use examples and other illustrative materials to explain unfamiliar concepts?

Does the TA show enthusiasm for the subject matter?

Does the TA direct class discussions fairly and effectively?

Does the TA invite and respond effectively to student questions?[5]

Classroom communication skills enable TAs to successfully implement their instructional designs.

Questions about TA Interpersonal Skills   TAs are expected to get along with their students on an interpersonal level. Some of the areas of interpersonal competence that TAs may wish to inquire about are suggested by the questions that follow:

Does the TA appear to be interested in you and your progress?

Does the TA treat you in a friendly and respectful manner?

Is the TA available for consultation outside of class?

Does the TA listen attentively when you seek help?

Do you look forward to interpersonal exchanges with the TA?[6]

When TAs are interpersonally insensitive to the needs, feelings, and interests of their students, negative reactions so inspired are often reflected across all categories on end-of-term evaluation forms.

Questions about TA Grading and Evaluation   Under the best of circumstances, students often feel that grading in a course or section is subjective and unfair. The extent to which a TA is having problems in this area can be determined by questions such as the following:

Are the TA's standards for grading and evaluation clearly delineated?

Are the TA's standards for grading and evaluation fairly applied?

Is the TA's evaluation of student work thorough and helpful?

Does the TA return papers and examinations "within a reasonable period of time"?[7]

Since negative feelings in this area can lead to end-of-term grade complaints and protests, TAs are well advised to secure student feedback at midterm or even earlier.

How to Ask Students about Your Teaching   Just as there are a number of questions that TAs may ask about their teaching, there are a number of formats through which such questions may be asked and answered. In this section, three formats for securing student feedback will be considered.

Invite Written Evaluations   Written evaluations have a number of advantages: most students are accustomed to providing course evaluations in this way; written evaluations are relatively anonymous; and written evaluations avoid direct confrontation and potential escalations of feelings. Finally, written evaluations, since they are not interactive, can focus attention on the exact questions the TA wishes students to address. Written evaluations often include rating scales. Questions such as those presented earlier are accompanied by a series of numbers (one through five or one through seven, commonly). At the top of the scales, the meaning to be assigned to each number is indicated.

In addition to or instead of using rating scales, TAs may also provide open-ended questions or open-ended sentence stems to invite student feedback. Some sample open-ended sentence stems follow:

The thing I like best about you as an instructor is. . . .

The thing I like least about you as an instructor is. . . .

I would like you to do more. . . .

I would like you to do less. . . .

In this class I feel best when. . . .

If I could change one thing in this class it would be. . . .[8]

Since student responses to open-ended questions or open-ended sentence stems are expressed in their own language, the depth of student feelings, both positive and negative, often emerges with great clarity. For example, the question "What can your TA do to improve the quality of instruction in this section?" was answered by a student in one section with the words, "Don't change a thing. This is the best section I have had at the university." A student in another section replied, "The TA talks too much, belittles student questions, and is unapproachable; he can improve this course by leaving the teaching profession." While negative evaluations can sting, they are better received on the TA's own evaluation form filled out early in the term than on a departmental end-of-term evaluation form.

Invite Oral Evaluations   One method TAs may use to gain student reactions to their teaching is to interview students informally as circumstances permit. Such interviews can be accomplished while walking with a student to or from class, during a chance encounter on or off campus, or in the TA's office at the end of a student visit. Some TAs make it a point to invite a student to have a cup of coffee for the express purpose of talking about "how things are going." The advantage that oral evaluations have over written evaluations is that the TA can ask students to sharpen their judgments and can secure specific advice by asking follow-up questions.

Another method of providing for oral evaluations is to form an advisory group. The group should be relatively small and should be a representative sample of the students in the class or section. The advisory group can meet with the TA during the first week of the term to discuss early student reactions to course or section goals and procedures. The group could continue to convene periodically to assess how things are going and to offer specific advice on such matters as "clarity of objectives, progress toward objectives, work load, teaching style, clarity and appropriateness of assignments, student interest and attitude, and other dimensions you consider important."[9]

Provide for Ongoing Evaluation   While periodic oral and written evaluations can provide a wealth of information, TAs may also use ongoing evaluative activities. One of these, the *telephone answering machine,* was discussed in chapter 6. Students wishing to offer reactions or suggestions can do so by calling the TA's home answering machine during designated hours.

Similarly, the Berkeley TA handbook suggests the *question box* as a means of obtaining feedback. TAs are advised to "bring a box or manilla envelope to class and ask students to place their unsigned comments, questions, or complaints in it."[10] As with the telephone answering machine, the question box will alert TAs to student problems and concerns as they arise. Such ongoing evaluations enable TAs to clear up little problems before they become big problems and to recognize major problems that must be resolved. These evaluative activities also suggest to students that their TA genuinely cares about them as individuals and cares about their reactions—both positive and negative.

Finally, TAs can benefit from periodically looking at student *class notes.*[11] After making an assignment, explaining a laboratory exercise, giving a mini-lecture or lecture, leading a class discussion, or conducting a review, TAs may ask permission to look at student notes. While cluttered, confused, or incomplete notes may be the result of poor note-taking by the student, should notes by several students reflect the same attributes, TAs may have cause to question the clarity and completeness of their presentations. To avoid seeming intrusive, TAs may provide handouts on which students are to complete a skeletal outline, record an assignment, or provide responses to questions as the TA talks. The handouts may then be collected, evaluated, and returned.

Securing Evaluations from Supervisors and Peers

Although many departments, and even entire universities, require that TAs be observed in classroom or laboratory settings, the number and nature of such observations vary dramatically. Some TAs are observed several times during the course of the semester while other TAs are observed just once or not at all during a term. Some universities provide printed multiple-copy forms for observers to use when recording and reacting to TA practices, while other institutions provide little or no guidance regarding what to look for or how to provide an evaluative response. In this section, three guidelines for inviting and profiting from the reactions of supervisors and peers will be considered.

TAs do not always look forward to classroom visits by supervisors or other TAs. Admittedly, an anticipated visit from an intelligent, informed adult can cause a TA's pulse to quicken. When such visits are mandated by department, college, or university policy, it is easy for the TA to feel more like the object of evaluation than a party to evaluation.

Welcome External Evaluation

Evaluations by supervisors and peers can, however, be a useful supplement to student evaluations. External observers, who are usually teachers themselves, are likely to notice things that escape the attention of students. And since external observers are not directly involved in the classroom, they can provide a more objective account of classroom events than students can.

When departments provide for such supervisory visits, TAs are given an opportunity to gain useful information about their teaching from a concerned other. When departments do not provide for observation, TAs may invite such visits on their own. Course directors are unlikely to refuse a TA's direct request to be visited and evaluated. TAs may also invite fellow TAs to observe their teaching and provide evaluative comments. Visits by peers are often less threatening to TAs than visits by course directors. It is also easier for peers to be forthright with each other when conferring about a visit.

In those cases where supervisors are expected to use standard evaluation forms, the TA may suggest additional questions for the observer to reflect upon. In cases where such forms are not used, the TA may prepare a longer list of topics she or he would like to discuss with the supervisor or peer in a postobservational conference. Fuhrmann and Grasha suggest a number of worthwhile questions that may be addressed by observers, including the following:

Identify Special Observational Foci

> Does the instructor have annoying mannerisms or other habits? . . .
>
> How long does it take discussion groups to get started? How much time do they spend on the topics assigned?
>
> Are students given interesting and challenging topics to discuss? What occurred to suggest the topics were interesting and challenging? What occurred to suggest that they were not?

Are the content presentations organized? Is this organization apparent to the student? How does the instructor let the student know about the organization for the session?

Are students talking about class content while they are entering or leaving class?

Do students take initiative in asking questions and trying to get issues discussed? What specific examples of behaviors suggest that this occurs? . . .

Does the instructor answer his or her own questions? If so, how often does this occur?

Are new terms defined for the students? Which terms were defined and which ones were not defined?

What are some of the things students are doing while the instructor is presenting or answering questions? Develop a list of them.

Does the instructor walk around during class or stay in one place? What effect does this have on the class?

Do students snicker or otherwise make fun of what the instructor says or does? What do they say or do? How often does this occur?

What types of visual aids are used? Are they appropriate for the level of the course and the students in the classroom?[12]

This potpourri of questions illustrates the broad array of issues that observers may address. When anticipating a visit from a supervisor or peer, the TA should choose questions that reflect his or her particular responsibilities, instructional practices, goals, and personal concerns.

Hold an Evaluative Conference

Following an observation a conference is normally scheduled at the earliest opportunity, while the period is still fresh in the minds of both TA and observer. During the conference, an attempt is made initially to *reconstruct and clarify what happened* during the observed period. The discussion often focuses on events rather than on judgments about events. Once a composite view of the period has been sketched, an attempt is made to *assign values to events;* in so doing, both positive and negative judgments are arrived at, hopefully through consensus. An attempt is then made to *identify areas of TA strength and weakness.* Beginning TAs have as much difficulty determining what they are doing right as what they are doing wrong. It is important, therefore, that conversation focus on strengths that the TA may exploit as well as on weaknesses that the TA may eliminate. Finally, the TA and observer often *explore means of improvement.* It is important that the TA have a chance to verbalize, and receive an evaluation of, possible avenues of self-improvement. While this portion of the conference is highly tentative, since the TA will find

An evaluation conference with the course director can help the TA identify areas of strength and weakness.

it necessary to experiment with a number of strategies over time, it provides a starting point for an ongoing program of personal growth and improvement.

In addition to securing feedback from students and supervisors or peers, TAs can become a valuable data source for themselves if they sharpen their awareness of classroom events. A popular communication axiom notes, "You can't not communicate," which is to say, one transmits messages whether or not one intends to do so. In the classroom student tardiness, inattention, frowns, yawns, and glassy-eyed stares all communicate one kind of message; student smiles, laughter, thoughtful looks, and active note-taking communicate quite another.

Engaging in Self-evaluation

A popular publication recently included the observation that "evidence that things are not going well in a class is difficult to miss, especially from the vantage point at the front of the room."[13] Yet many college instructors—professors and TAs alike—*do* miss signs that all is not well. So how can TAs become more attuned to positive and negative classroom events?

Monitoring Classroom Events

Attend to Student Verbal and Nonverbal Messages   It is very easy for TAs to attend to the cognitive aspects of the classroom at the expense of affective aspects. After all, TAs have readings to review, information to explain, demonstrations to perform, assignments to make, and tests to return and discuss. There seems to be little time left for worrying about affect. Still, affect—student feelings about the instructor, course content, and class procedures—can strongly influence cognitive learning. Without losing sight of cognitive goals, TAs can increase their awareness of student expressions of affect through both verbal and nonverbal means. On a given day a TA may make a special effort to note student reactions:

> What do students do before the class period begins? Do they engage each other in social interaction? Do they engage you in social interaction? Do they talk about course content or work? Do they ignore you and each other in favor of reading the campus newspaper?

> How do students react to initial class activities? Do they put the campus paper away and prepare to take notes? Do they grumble or look disgusted during your preview of the period? Do they show enthusiasm for an upcoming assignment you discuss?

> Do students act in desired ways during the period? Do students listen carefully to lectures? Are your periodic queries about lecture content correctly answered? Are most of the students actively involved in whole-class discussions? Are students task oriented in small-group activities? Do students show enthusiasm for laboratory experiments?

> How do the students relate to you? Do they use your name when addressing you? Do they approach you personally to ask questions and advice about assignments? Do they visit you during office hours?

> What positive and negative sentiments are expressed by students? What words do they use to describe you, the course, course materials, or learning activities? What nonverbal messages are conveyed by student facial expressions, eye contact, gestures, or posture?

As TAs become more aware of student verbal and nonverbal messages, they can also become more responsive to student needs and interests.

Attend to Your Own Verbal and Nonverbal Messages   In addition to monitoring student messages, TAs will also wish to monitor their own communications. Among the questions TAs may wish to ask about themselves are the following:

> Do I show respect for my students? Do I avoid attributing negative qualities to them? (e.g.,"I don't suppose you've started your papers yet"). Do I respond to wrong answers in class discussions in a non-punitive way? Do I offer criticism in a private and constructive manner? Do I avoid sarcasm?

Do I show respect for humankind? Do I avoid statements, examples, stories, and asides that are racist, sexist, or otherwise demeaning? Do I demonstrate a high regard for the rights of all people?

Do I show enthusiasm for the course I am teaching? Do I indicate the importance of the subject matter? Do I avoid negative comments about the course, the course director, and course materials and procedures?

Do I communicate information in a clear, accurate, and interesting manner? Are my presentations well organized? Are my examples clear and relevant? Does my oral delivery enhance my verbal message? Does my physical behavior contribute to or distract from the content being considered?

Do I take a personal interest in my students and their work? Do I address them by name? Do I seem friendly and approachable? Do I welcome questions? Do I provide praise and encouragement when such responses are appropriate?

Sensitivity to self is an important ingredient in effective teaching. TAs who are not aware of what they are communicating to others may seem aloof, disinterested, hostile, preoccupied, and arrogant without even knowing it.

Since it is sometimes difficult to conduct a class or section while, at the same time, being aware of all the subtle nuances of meaning that are being communicated, it is often useful to audiotape or videotape class meetings for subsequent analysis. Audiotapes, while having the advantages of being easy to make and convenient to replay, exclude a good deal of information that the visual image conveys. For this reason, many universities have educational media centers with personnel who will videotape class meetings in the comfort of the TA's own laboratory or classroom. Such videotapes come much closer to capturing the full range of events that transpired during a period than do audiotapes. To maximize the usefulness of the videotape, it is important that the camera operator be asked to record student reactions and small-group interactions as well as your presentation.

Reviewing Audiotapes and Videotapes

When viewing the videotape, the full range of questions considered earlier in this section may be addressed. In addition, the camera will catch other kinds of events that escaped you when they occurred live in the classroom or laboratory. For example, you may notice that students try to avoid eye contact when you are asking questions, that some students aren't speaking loudly enough to be heard by all the other students when responding to your questions (and thus should have their answers repeated by you), that students are whispering to each other more than

Videotapes of class meetings enable TAs to test their perceptions of classroom events.

you had noticed, that you aren't always aware that students are trying to get your attention, that you don't wait long enough for students to respond to your questions before moving on to other students, that the students are delighted when you build their names into your examples and illustrations, or that you pace a good deal while talking.[14]

Charting a Course for Improvement

Throughout the first three sections of this chapter, it has been suggested that TAs gather evaluative data throughout the term rather than waiting for institutionally prescribed end-of-term evaluations. By so doing, TAs can begin a program of improvement well before the end-of-term evaluations are administered. Furthermore, such self-motivated evaluations let you "ask the questions about teaching that most interest you. Because you make these key decisions, you tend to look at the feedback more seriously, which will probably increase its impact on your instruction."[15] In this final section, four stages in the process of teaching growth will be charted.

Recognizing the Need for Improvement

Those who have worked with TAs extensively often marvel at the improvements in teaching abilities they have witnessed. In some cases the change "has taken as little as a student small-group evaluation that pointed out minor defects in questioning technique or grading policy," whereas in other cases the change "has required considerable time learning better methods of organization or delivery."[16] Whatever the time and effort required, "the crucial factor in each case has been the teacher's willingness to recognize the need to change and to invest the time necessary to learn new skills."[17]

Unfortunately, even in the face of substantial negative evidence, TAs sometimes deny the need for teaching improvement. To preserve their sense of self-esteem, they look elsewhere for explanations by claiming that the evaluation instrument asks the wrong questions, or that their evaluations are lower than those of other TAs because their standards are higher, or that the particular teaching assistantship position is too demanding and no one could do it well, or that the course director, the textbook, the syllabus, or the instructional approach is hopelessly flawed.

Having accepted the fact that there is room for improvement, TAs must next determine which particular areas of teaching are most in need of change. Students' evaluations can be helpful in this regard. If a rating scale is used, the TA may compute a mean score for each evaluative question for each section taught. The TA may then identify areas that receive low evaluations and can compare mean scores across sections to verify that different sections of students have identified the same shortcomings. In interpreting student responses to open-ended questions, the TA should search for patterns of critical comments. Similar comments should be recorded in clusters by the TA. By naming each cluster, the TA can facilitate comparisons across sections and can begin to identify a manageable number of areas for improvement.

Identifying Areas for Improvement

After analyzing available data, TAs can profit from discussing their findings with others. The course director may be able to provide insights regarding the areas of concern students have expressed. Students may be able to validate concerns expressed by the course supervisor or peers. Conclusions drawn from self-evaluations, either in class or on videotape, may be validated through discussions with students, peers, or both.

One leading book on college teaching, written for professors, recommends that instructors identify in writing the changes they intend to implement in their teaching. Such written records may be seen as self-contracts—promissory notes pointing the direction for self-improvement.[18] While the forms recommended are sometimes complex, they need not be. For example, a TA may simply identify perceived problems and a number of strategies for coping with the problems.

Determining Improvement Strategies

Statement of Perceived Problem	Possible Solutions
1. Students feel that grades are unfair.	1a. Describe grading policies, both orally and in writing, during the first class meeting.
	1b. Prepare criteria sheets for each major project, indicating what a student must do to earn an A, B, etc.
	1c. Distribute "ideal" essay question answers when each exam is returned.
2. Course supervisor alleges that the pacing of sections is slow.	2a. Begin class promptly.
	2b. Ensure that introductory activities take no longer than five minutes.
	2c. Ask students with personal concerns to stop by after class.
	2d. Write time goals on the left-hand margin of the plan for each session and pay attention to them.
3. Students complain that assignments and explanations are often unclear.	3a. Use the chalkboard, handouts, and other audio/visual materials to supplement explanations.
	3b. Ask students direct questions to test their comprehension of directions and explanations.
	3c. Use more examples.
	3d. Ensure that new terms are defined as they are introduced.

As this example suggests, it is important that TAs focus on a limited number of problems at a time in order that the focus of improvement not be blurred. It is also important that improvement strategies be both well defined and attainable.

A plan for improvement must, of course, be flexible. When strategies prove inadequate to the task, new strategies must be devised and tested. When strategies prove effective, they should be incorporated into future teaching efforts. The interesting thing about teaching is that one may never rest on one's laurels. Each new course and each new term pose new challenges.

Teaching assistantships are sometimes viewed as professorial apprenticeships. This notion is not without merit. Just as cobblers and blacksmiths once learned their trades through on-the-job training, TAs learn how to teach college students by teaching. The value of this comparison lies in the realization that an apprenticeship is a time of growth. Just as no one expected a fledgling cobbler to fashion a perfect shoe, no one should expect a fledgling TA to teach a perfect class. The TA should, however, experience growth as the years of graduate study unfold. The Stanford guide advises that "new assistant professors are expected to assume and be successful at multiple roles—teacher, researcher, university citizen—very quickly. If you already know how to prepare courses, deliver lectures, conduct discussions, and all the rest, then you will have more time for publishing and university service."[19]

While growing in knowledge and research competence as a graduate student, each individual should experience commensurate growth as a teacher. In order to do so, TAs must be self-reflective throughout their years as teaching assistants and must take advantage of opportunities for personal teaching growth. One means of self-reflection and growth is to keep a teaching journal. One resource on college teaching recommends that, at the end of each session, instructors take a few "quick notes about how the class session went. Identify sections that were or were not smooth, places where you need examples, questions students asked and you did or did not answer well, how the activities were received, the idea for a test question that came to you during the lecture, or any other impressions that linger in your mind."[20] It is also suggested that instructors list "the three things that most need to be done to improve this day in class."[21]

Another strategy for promoting growth is to visit the classes of other TAs. When visiting the sections of other TAs in the same course, TAs may glean ideas and methods that may be used immediately in their own teaching. Visits to the classes or sections of TAs in other courses can enrich one's own teaching experience and provide ideas for both present and future teaching encounters. Such visits are also useful since they are likely to promote dialogue among TAs about teaching. The Harvard guide suggests that interacting with peers "is certainly one of the best ways to improve your teaching" and that "you will be well repaid for any time and energy you contribute to organizing such conversations."[22]

Still another strategy for improvement is to arrange to be videotaped periodically in order that you may judge your teaching progress over time. Such videotapes may also provide the stimulus for discussions with the course director or other TAs about teaching.

The strategies advanced here are merely suggestions. The point being made is that TAs should experience teaching growth across the years of apprenticeship. In order for this to happen, TAs must be self-reflective and must chart a course for personal improvement by seizing all available opportunities for growth. The ultimate rationale for improvement was provided by Lowman when he noted that "instructors should . . . strive [for] excellent classroom teaching because it is more rewarding to do anything well than to accept mediocrity" and because "every great teacher decided to work at mastering [the teacher's] art for the very personal reason that being a virtuoso in the classroom is so inherently rewarding."[23]

Summary

"Teaching is a learning process . . . a learnable skill, not an innate gift." For this reason, TAs should perceive their appointments as opportunities for growth. Student feedback helps point the direction for such improvement. TAs may question students regarding their perceptions of the TA's overall effectiveness, planning skills, classroom communication skills, interpersonal skills, and grading practices. Such student feedback may be invited through written evaluations, oral evaluations, and ongoing evaluative activities. Evaluations from supervisors and peers are also useful. In order to profit from such advice, TAs must welcome external evaluations, provide descriptive information, identify special observational foci, and arrange for an evaluative conference. TAs may also engage in thoughtful self-evaluation by monitoring the verbal and nonverbal messages of students and themselves both live in classroom settings and through reviewing audiotapes and videotapes. To grow through teaching, TAs can chart a course for improvement by recognizing the need for improvement, identifying areas for improvement, determining improvement strategies, and seizing opportunities for teaching growth. TAs should recognize that a teaching assistantship is a professorial apprenticeship through which they may acquire teaching competence and the inherent rewards that accompany being a successful teacher.

Notes

1. *Teaching Fellows Handbook* (Cambridge, Mass.: Harvard-Danforth Center for Teaching and Learning, 1986–87), p. 38.
2. Libby Wood, "Discussion Sections in the Sciences," in *Learning to Teach: A Handbook for Teaching Assistants at U.C. Berkeley* (Berkeley: Graduate Assembly, University of California, 1985), p. 19.
3. These four objectives parallel objectives 1, 2, 3, and 11 in Gerald M. Meredith and Todd G. Ogasawia, "Scale for Excellence in Teaching Award for Teaching Assistants," *Perceptual and Motor Skills* 53 (1981): 633–34.
4. The writing of two of the objectives in this grouping were influenced by a Department of Communication Arts Course Evaluation Form at the University of Wisconsin–Madison, March 1985.
5. The objectives in this set are based in part on the work of Meredith and Ogasawia and on the Wisconsin Communication Arts Form.

6. The objectives in this set were also influenced by the sources identified in the previous note with the stronger influence provided by Meredith and Ogasawia.

7. The objectives in this set were excerpted from the Wisconsin Communication Arts Form.

8. Barbara Schneider Fuhrmann and Anthony F. Grasha, *A Practical Handbook for College Teachers* (Boston: Little, Brown and Company, 1983), p. 197.

9. Fuhrmann and Grasha, p. 203.

10. Barbara Davis, "Evaluating Your Teaching," in *Learning to Teach,* p. 62.

11. This recommendation is made by both Davis, p. 62, and Fuhrmann and Grasha, p. 203.

12. Barbara Schneider Fuhrmann and Anthony F. Grasha, *A Practical Handbook for College Teachers* (Boston: Little, Brown and Company, 1983), p. 210. Used with permission.

13. *The Teaching Professor* 2 (June, 1988): 2.

14. Some of the ideas that are enumerated in this paragraph were suggested by *Notes for TA Consultants* (Los Angeles: University of California at Los Angeles, 1984), pp. 183–85.

15. *The Teaching Professor*, p. 1.

16. Michele Fisher, ed., *Teaching at Stanford: An Introductory Handbook*, rev. ed. (Stanford, Calif.: Center for Teaching and Learning, Stanford University, 1983), p. 21.

17. Fisher, p. 21.

18. Fuhrmann and Grasha, p. 218.

19. Fisher, p. 28.

20. *The Teaching Professor*, p. 2.

21. *The Teaching Professor,* p. 2.

22. *Teaching Fellows Handbook,* p. 37.

23. Joseph Lowman, *Mastering the Techniques of Teaching* (San Francisco: Jossey-Bass, 1984), pp. 226–27.

Index